SUBTITLES

**BICYCLE THIEVES
Director: Ronzoni Barretti**

Ricci! A job for you!

Do you have a bicycle?

I have one, just not now.

I'll sell all our high thread count sheets...

...and get your Huffy out of hock.

It's my new job!

STOP, THIEF!

Look for your bicycle in the market, loser.

That's my Huffy!

Did you have a Hello Kitty bell on your bike? Loser!

LOOK! There's the thief with that old man!

Where does the thief live?

HANDS OFF, LOSER!

Dad, look, the thief!

You stole my Huffy!

You got proof? Loser! Get lost!

I'll steal someone's Huffy! (SOUND OF BELL)

THIEF! GRAB HIM!

**THE END
Dad, you're such a loser.**

GOODBYE, MR. CHIPS

Please forgive the length; I miss my friend and want to spend as much time with him as I can.

As some of you know, our dear Sean Kelly died this past July. It is now December, and I still can't write about it. Issue #24 has been on my desk for six solid weeks, finished in full except for this one damn piece. Now, the printer's telling me I've got to ship files *today* to have any chance of hitting Dec. 31.

If Sean were here, he could do it—with ease and charm and a level of erudition that would make you question if you'd ever truly read anything at all. But Sean is not here, and that is the problem.

I can't do it.

I won't do it.

If I don't write this, maybe it will un-happen. Maybe Sean will call tomorrow and say it was all a joke, a trick to unmask "The Bone" (Tony Hendra), or prise away some back pay from Matty Simmons.

If anything is stronger than Death, it's how Sean felt about Matty and The Bone. If by some slim chance those three are housed in the same place, God will most definitely not get back His deposit.

From SK to MG: I have a story concerning Brian and his immortal Mr Peanut comic I must share with you sometime.

Thanks to some faceless factotum at AOL looking to save server space, my entire professional life between 1994 and 2005 has been relegated to folk-memory. But circumstantial evidence suggests that I met Sean around 1995, when I was writing a doomed history of American comedy for St. Martin's. Sean was at his best: warm, forthright and hilarious. He told me to steer clear of Tony and Matty—I did—and gave me my first entrée into that peculiar clan. Maneuvering among the Lampooners took delicacy, but having grown up in an alcoholic family, it was second nature. Through Sean, I met the glorious Alice Playten (RIP), hilarious Garry Goodrow (RIP), and…maybe you're noticing a trend?

Who signed off on this? It's monstrous. I don't think anyone should have to live in a world without these people in it. I don't think I want to.

Oh, well. Let's give it until the end of this piece.

In 1996, I sent Sean *The Bull Street Journal* (see *Bystander* #21), and he was very complimentary, much more than I or the project deserved. Though people like Doug Kenney got more ink, Sean Kelly was one of the top parodists of his parody-crazy generation; Brian McConnachie called Sean "*The Lampoon's* Gilbert *and* Sullivan," and I think Brian was right. Sean's spoofery was notable enough to land him on the cover of *Newsweek*. Those of you who weren't around for "magazines," imagine Twitter, only much slower, much less crazy, and everybody got paid for their tweets. There were no Nazis, unless you counted *The National Review*. It was a world of wonder, possibility, and cigarette ads, where porn was still kind of an occasion and people got famous *for writing parodies*. That's all gone now, just like Sean. Now we have Elon and Tik Tok. *Is diss a system?* (That's the kind of reference Sean would've enjoyed.)

From SK to MG: There isn't anything I would enjoy in a vertical position more than a conversation with your noble self anywhere on any subject.

During those early years, Sean and I would mostly gab about his older kids, Chris and Erin, both of whom were (are) so smart and funny it's kind of sickening. Or of Mack, his younger son.

"How's Mack?"

"He just pitched a shutout."

"Another one? Sean, forgive me, but who *does* that?"

"I know," he said. "It comes from Trish's side."

We might touch on the doings of our various mutuals, or discuss an essential question of the day, like Was Doug Kenney gay? or Was Michael O'Donoghue taking heroin for his migraines and/or into BDSM? Gossip about the dead—good clean fun.

I once screwed up my courage and asked it. "What's your beef with Tony, anyway?"

Though the proximate cause had been Tony's swiping of the book deal for *Going Too Far*—"He took the advance, then wrote the second half of the book on cocaine." "He did seem to be hurrying," I quipped—Sean's disagreement was philosophical. "Tony, like the Catholic seminarian he once was, is determined to prove the existence of evil. If necessary," Sean said, "he'll do it himself."

In these bull sessions, we also complained about the comedy business, me mostly from the outside. Apart from *The Onion*, I wasn't seeing a lot of the kind of comedy that had set my brains ablaze in the Seventies, and to have Sean confirm that, yes, it wasn't just the references that had changed was reassuring. Maybe not helpful as far as getting work was concerned, but still. Sean and I both loathed what he called "Now, This"— "A joke about Abu Ghraib, now a joke about Madonna's cone bra, now a joke about the Pope being a virgin, now a joke about Chinese factory workers throwing themselves out windows after making your iPhone."

MICHAEL GERBER (@mgerber937) is Editor & Publisher of *The American Bystander*.

"Now, This" repels the very idea of discernment, elevating the unimportant and diminishing the truly shocking. It feels like intelligence, but in fact it's snipping the wires connecting satire to…anything, really. All reality is ground into the same powder, to be snorted for whatever thrill it can give. "All fame, no shame," Sean said. Excellent soil, we concluded later, for the sprouting of a Trump.

Sean liked my *Harry Potter* parody because, in the grand tradition of satire, it was actually pissed off about something. He read the manuscript and pronounced it "perfect." If Sean hadn't encouraged me, I might've junked it; I was 32, about to be married, and expecting a lawsuit from Scholastic, Warner Bros., J.K. Rowling, or all three. The risk was only worth it if the book was *good*.

"Publish it. You must."

"Is it too broad?"

"No such thing," Sean said. "We're talking about smart 12-year-olds here."

Sean blurbed it, and later Trish published it for S&S. *Barry Trotter* scratched my name into the pediment of lit'ry greats—at least for six months or so—and I'm grateful to them both to this day. Once, during Barry-mania, I forwarded Sean a copy of *The London Times* list. He wrote back, "This week, *Barry Trotter* jumps Alice Sebold's *Lovely Bones*!"

WIPE THAT LEAR OFF YOUR FACE
The Pubble that has no dong
Once had one excessively vast;
But his nautical uncle one runcible time
Took it off with a mixture of beeswax and lime,
To use on his boat for a mast,
(An act which was morally wrong)…

[several complete poems followed]

Stuff like the above flowed into my inbox with regularity, so ten years later, Sean was one of the first people I turned to when *Bystander* began. The piece he and Rick Meyerowitz contributed to Issue #2, "Birds of Prey," remains one of my favorites. As with *Barry Trotter*, their support showed me that there was something here worth fighting for.

As the magazine began to take shape—and I began writing stuff in a much different register than I had prior to my illness—Sean saw the change and encouraged it.

A BEATNIK FAMILY PORTRAIT: *Sean, Norma, Erin, Chris, and the baby Siobhan, circa 1965.*

From SK to MG: Dear Sir, texts like your Christmas Memory benefit all living things. Yours in awe—

The best kind of mentor acts like an Uncle—someone who loves you, but isn't responsible for you, and the space between their person and The Law allows them to take a wider view of Life and how you might live it. This Uncle teaches you how to play blackjack, precisely because he's not on the hook for your debts. As a nod to Life's responsibilities, however, he might just teach you how to cheat.

There was something of the Uncle in Sean, and I loved it. "Sean, we've got a good thing here. You and I enjoy the pleasure of affinity without the burden of genetics."

Sean agreed; the next time I heard from him it was two words on Facebook: "miss you."

(Looking at it now, I notice it was the 41st anniversary of John Lennon's murder. Sean knew that John is one of my guys, and one of his guys too, so maybe he was missing John. Or us both. There were usually multiple meanings going on with Sean; they felt like puzzles with compliments at the end.)

From SK to MG: Endangered Species Poem

Ursus maritimus
The Coney Island Polar Bear Club is the oldest
winter bathing organization in the United States.

Puma concolor coryi
Florida Panthers
and floridapanthers.com
are trademarks of the Florida Panthers
Hockey Club, Ltd.

Gymnogyps
The Condor
Club in San Francisco is the birthplace of the world's first topless & bottomless entertainment.

Aniyunwiya
& then, there's the Jeep Cherokee.

In any sane world, Sean would've been installed inside some posh uni somewhere, and spent the rest of his life as a turned-on, tuned-in Mr. Chips. What died in July wasn't just a person, but a body of knowledge, a relationship to the past and the present, a whole world, really. That species of human—*Homo literatus satirica*—is gone, and not coming back.

Here in America, most comedy writers don't know much outside of showbiz. Sean, on the other hand, knew everything. He was the most fiercely literate person I've ever met. He was what I hoped to find in the New York publishing business. He was the Platonic ideal of the man holding court in the pub.

People told me Sean could be cutting, and when you spoke to him you felt the atmospheric pressure of that immense analytical brain. I am sure Sean knew all my fears and foibles, my secret lusts and motivations, better than I did. But he never, not once, said anything unkind to me. In fact, he was endlessly supportive, endlessly charitable, endlessly encouraging as I generated one harebrained scheme after the other, including this magazine.

Sean was writing a memoir, and every once in a while I'd get a piece extracted from it. The last one, on page 43, was slated for #22, but I had to shuffle it forward. Now that he's dead, I suppose I can run it for free. I can hear Sean now: "Matty would be proud."

The last time I saw Sean was April of 2019, at the last big *Bystander* lunch before COVID. As some of you know, we periodically cram ourselves into the back room of Joanne's, an Italian restaurant on 68th Street where my partner Alan knows the owner. I'm always a bit nervous about these events—a single gas leak could wipe out the entire magazine—but have no time to worry, circulating about the room with a handshake and a smile and apologies for how little we paid last time and how next time it will be more. (It never is.) The contributors play along, and try to make up what they can in free pizza and lasagna and wine.

These afternoons are intense. Normally, I sit out here in Santa Monica, loving and appreciating everyone so much, often for years at a time, and now we're all together and THEY MUST BE TOLD. That I loved a piece, loved a drawing, love them. And yes, that piece you sent is still in the lineup, sorry, something timely came in right as we were going to press. I have to pack a whole year's worth of Publisher-ing into four hours. The last time we had one of these, Jenny Boylan walked over to me. Taking me by the arm, she said, "Sit down. Have a glass of water. Brian and I are worried you're working too hard." I sat down—when Jenny speaks, I listen…

then asked, "I heard you wrote a song for the *Bystander.*" Jenny sang it to me.

Thus refreshed, I went back into the fray, doing what I was designed by God and St. Louis tavern culture to do.

So there I am, smiling, jiving, sweating through my tweeds—literally pinned into a corner by people and jokes and affection—and someone said, "Sean's here."

…AAAND AWAY WE GO!: *Sean cutting up with his youngest son Mac, around 2000.*

"Sean? WHERE?"

"Over there, by Brian."

"Excuse me pardon me excuse me pardon me"—the staffers part, showing me a respect unknown in the rest of my life—and there Sean stands, a little more stooped, a little grayer, but recognizably the dear man.

"UNCLE SEAN!" I yell. He is pleased. We hug. "Thanks so much for coming."

"I couldn't miss it."

"Well, you could've." Last phone call Sean told me he'd been suffering from a bit of agoraphobia, which I also struggle with. "But I'm so so glad you didn't."

He smiles. "Quite a crowd."

"Wouldn't have happened without you. You kept me going when I was a kid."

"You were talented."

"When every door was closed, you'd remind me of that. It meant so much."

"We showed 'em," Sean said.

"Let's drink to that! What do you want, red or white?" I picked up an empty carafe. "I'll go find some, I'll be back."

"I'll be here," Sean said. But on the way, someone grabbed my sleeve and started pitching me, and by the time I extricated myself from that and returned with a glass of red and a glass of white—I'd drink whatever Sean didn't prefer—Sean was gone.

"Where'd Sean go?" I asked Alan.

"He had to leave." I understood. That room was small and crowded. I knew what it had taken for him to come, and be there.

I was genuinely sad, and Brian saw it. "Until the next time."

"I know," I said. "I just wish I'd gotten a chance to say goodbye."

From SK to MG: Michael, your friendship has been the most pleasant experience in my dotage. Convey my best wishes to St. Kate.

I have no doubt Sean Kelly ended up in Heaven. Here's my proof: a year and a half ago, my wife was coming out of major surgery. We're sitting together in the recovery room, and she's in the twilight state. Coming out of unconsciousness, the first thing Kate says is: "…Sean Kelly."

I laughed so loud the nurse looked over. "Dear, did you just say 'Sean Kelly'?"

Kate doesn't answer. After a while she says, "More ice chips."

Sean and Kate never met, but I talked a lot about each to the other; they were cut from the same cloth, both Jesuits, or as I call them, "the Jews of Catholicism." I think the two of them met in the waiting room of Heaven that evening, Kate passing through, Sean maybe filling out some final paperwork so things would go smoothly when the time came.

I don't know whether Sean believed in Heaven, I only know he earned it. And I don't know whether he believed in all those Saints either, but whenever I'm stuck on a piece, I'll ask for his help. It worked this time.

Thanks, Sean. For everything. Goodbye. **B**

TABLE OF CONTENTS

DEPARTMENTS

GALLIMAUFRY

Tracey Berglund, Jenn Knott, David DeGrand, Melissa Balmain, James Finn Garner, Chris Galletta, Raven Burnett, Richard Seltzer, Julien Perez, Nick Mullins, Chris Spark, Craig Whitaker, Mat Barton, Adam Cooper, David Saliterman, Jon Zeller.

SHORT STUFF

The AMERICAN BYSTANDER

Founded 1981 by Brian McConnachie
#24 • Vol. 6, No. 4 • December 2022

EDITOR & PUBLISHER
Michael Gerber
HEAD WRITER Brian McConnachie
SENIOR EDITOR Alan Goldberg
DEPUTY EDITOR Michael Pershan
ORACLE Steve Young
STAFF LIAR P.S. Mueller
INTREPID TRAVELER Mike Reiss
EAGLE EYES Patrick L. Kennedy
AGENTS OF THE 2ND BYSTANDER INT'L
Eve Alintuck, Melissa Balmain, Ron Barrett, Roz Chast, Rick Geary, Sam Gross
MANAGING EDITOR EMERITA
Jennifer Finney Boylan
CONSIGLIERA Kate Powers
COVER BY HAUGE

ISSUE CONTRIBUTORS
Melissa Balmain, Mat Barton, Tracey Berglund, Barry Blitt, George Booth, M.K. Brown, Raven Burnett, Shawn Cheng, Tyson Cole, Adam Cooper, David DeGrand, Ivan Ehlers, Darryl Fefee, Chris Galletta, James Finn Garner, Lance Hansen, Quentin Hardy, Ron Hauge, Len Hawkins, Michelle Hlubinka, Tim Hunt, John Jonik, Sean Kelly, Jenn Knott, Jeff Kulik, Annelisa Leinbach, Richard Littler, Michael Lodato, Glenn Marshall, Steve McGinn, Sarah Morrissette, Nick Mullins, Ben Orlin, Julien Perez, Asher Perlman, Jon Plotkin, K.A. Polzin, David Saliterman, Richard Seltzer, Mike Shear, Jim Siergey, Mark Silverstein, Chris Spark, Rich Sparks, Nick Spooner, Craig Whitaker, Matt Wiegle, Mark Winter (Chicane), B.A. Van Sise, Jon Zeller.

Lanky Bareikis; Laura Sweet; Jon Schwarz; Alleen Schultz, Gray & Bernstein; Karen Backus; Lopez, Ivanhoe & Gumenick; Greg & Trish; and The Sheridan Press.
NAMEPLATES BY Mark Simonson
ISSUE CREATED BY Michael Gerber

FEATURES

OUR BACK PAGES

CARTOONS & ILLUSTRATIONS BY

Ron Hauge, Rich Sparks, Sam Gross, Tracey Berglund, David DeGrand, Nick Mullins, Craig Whitaker, Cooper & Barton, David Saliterman, Lance Hansen, Annelisa Leinbach, Jonathan Plotkin, Michelle Hlubinka, M.K. Brown, Len Hawkins, Mark Silverstein, John Jonik, Tim Hunt, Mark Winter (Chicane), Steve McGinn.

Sam's Spot

"I am going to pray for you."

COVER

RON HAUGE has an uncommon gift, one that comes from his million-horsepower brain: cartoons so stripped down and primal, they practically work on the subconscious. I'm just glad he's on the side of the good guys! When he showed me this one, I knew we had to have it. First of many, Ron.

ACKNOWLEDGMENTS

All material is ©2022 its creators, all rights reserved. Please do not reproduce or distribute any of it without written consent of the creators and *The American Bystander*. The following material has previously appeared, and is reprinted here with permission of the author(s): "Woe Unto Us," "How Six Made Good" and "Burbank, We Have a Problem" originally appeared in *The Yale Record 150th Anniversary Issue*, which you should buy via Amazon.com.

---◆---

THE AMERICAN BYSTANDER, *Vol. 6, No. 4*, (979-8-218-22130-0). Publishes ~4x/year. ©2022 by Good Cheer LLC. No part of this magazine can be reproduced, in whole or in part, by any means, without the written permission of the Publisher. For this and other queries, email Publisher@americanbystander.org, or write: Michael Gerber, Publisher, *The American Bystander*, 1122 Sixth St., #403, Santa Monica, CA 90403. Mags & merch can be purchased at www.americanbystander.org/store. **Subscribe at www.patreon.com/bystander.** More info? Check out www.americanbystander.org. We blog on Substack at www.theamericanbystander.substack.com. Whoever you are, thanks for reading.

Little
MEDUSA
THE FRIENDLY GORGON
GEE ...
I JUST WANTED
TO BE THEIR
FRIEND!
RAINY
DAY
WOMEN
#12 & 35
SIERGEY

BY MICHAEL PERSHAN

A TIME OF CELEBRATION

Another excerpt from Bialistock & Jones' 1976 photo essay on America, **Give Life Unto the Image of the Beast.**

You wouldn't know it from his dirty vest or crumpled ascot, but writer **Nachum Bialistock** *(1945-1976)* came from immense wealth. Son of a powerful deli magnate, he was educated at Exeter and Harvard. He spoke a heavily accented Brahmin Yiddish. He could enter any Upper West Side shop and walk out with complimentary pastrami.

In 1967 he presented himself at *Bystander*'s Grove Street offices, believing he was beginning an unpaid internship at *Ramparts*. Famously parsimonious, Publisher Arnold Gerber said nothing, and by the time Bialistock realized his error eight years later, he was *Bystander*'s unpaid Managing Editor and Gerber had saved over $42,000 on lunches.

To keep the enraged Bialistock from quitting, Gerber wrangled an impossibly fat Federal contract to document the lives of working-class Americans, and gave the assignment to Bialstock. The disheveled deli scion was jubilant. But this "dream job" would change Bialistock—and his country— forever.

Bialistock was, his friends attest, a deeply patriotic liberal with a spiritual bent; he spoke often about the nation as a living, breathing organism. Cities, for Bialistock, were the restless hands and feet of the body politic. Suburbs were the elbows, useless but essential. But the soul of the nation, Bialistock was apt to shout over drinks, were the honest, simple people who labored in factories, worshipped in churches, married young, had children, and died where they were born, ideally in the very same room.

Joined by photographer **Phyllis "Flip" Jones** *(1943-1976)* Bialistock set off in search of this national soul. They went to towns in New Jersey, Connecticut, Vermont, and New Hampshire. What they found, according to Bialistock's notes, was "a lot of disturbing sex stuff." So they traveled deeper into America's heartland, to Ohio, Iowa, Wisconsin, and Missouri.

If Bialistock was disturbed by what he saw in Connecticut, boy oh boy, did Iowa ever do a number on him. America, he was learning, was indeed made of generous men and women who weren't afraid to get their hands dirty. But not at all the way Bialistock had imagined.

Nachum Bialistock returned a different man. On July 4th, 1976, he arrived back at Grove Street smartly dressed, with a patterned ascot and a freshly-ironed vest with pastrami stuffed in his pockets. Without a word, he dropped off the manuscript, turned on his heel, and left. An unpaid intern saw him step into a limousine, and speed off into the New York night. Bialistock was never heard from again. What had happened? Only his words, and Jones' images, can tell the story.

"Now tell me Rebecca, have you been a good little girl this year?" **DEREK CHAVRAU**, *Beckley, WV, Appalachian Santa*

"And if the person responsible for this admits it of their own volition, I swear I will pray to God for your forgiveness." **REVEREND CALVIN**, *Newton, IA, on the condom on the altar*

"I believe we have a sacred duty to remember what we have lost, and I have lost so much." **ISAAC CHERBONYL,** *Lynn, MA, on his missing photographs*

"CIA, FBI, Havana, Moscow, I don't care who you work for: stop putting thoughts about Joey in my dreams!" **JOHNNY MASLOW,** *Peoria, IA, to the microphone in his casserole*

"A runaway teen named Suzie Macnamera? Doesn't ring a bell. Then again I'm an adult clown so our paths wouldn't necessarily have crossed." **SUZIE MACNAMERA,** *Rome, NY, unprompted*

"I did it! I did it, Momma! The fastest ever! And I think she liked it!" **PETER BROOKS,** *champion pig-fucker*

"Tell you what, there's more where that came from," **TREVOR LAKE**, *River, IN, on river shit*

"Tourism is up, that's the good news. You ready for the bad news?" **MAYOR DERRY** of *Acipco, AL, on his "Vodkaland" initiative*

"You're the guy who sold a dolphin to my grandma! That poor thing barely fit in the bathtub! What are we supposed to do with the body?" **MAYA WEST**, *Pittsburgh, PA, to a liar*

"I was skeptical at first, but I started seeing results pretty much immediately."
MARILYNE ADDISON, *Allstone, VA, on local tap water*

"Sure, I've got all the credentials back at home. Now who the fuck are you and who do you work for?" **DAISY FITZGERALD**, *Butler, WI, daycare operator*

"Dudes! I am so excited right now! That concussions are safe! Because that game! Was concussion city!"
TOMMY DENKINS, *before vomiting* **B**

MICHAEL PERSHAN *lays low in Brooklyn, NY.*

Gallimaufry

by Jenn Knott & David DeGrand

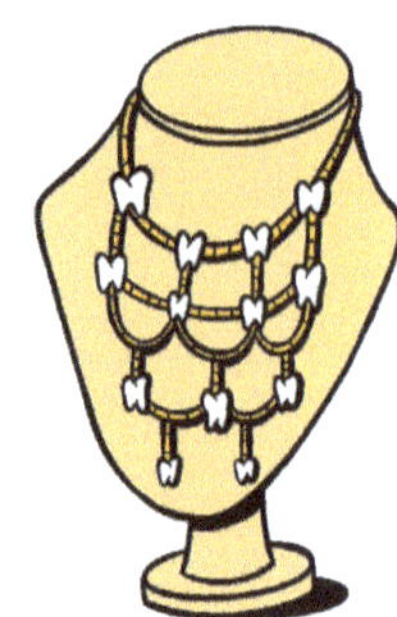
Unique Costume Jewelry

Non-toxic Pie Weights

Reusable Confetti (perfect for weddings!)

Miniature Scrabble Tiles

THE FIVE AGES OF WOMAN.

I. I howl like a brute
and befoul my pink suit
but the grownups declare that I'm dainty
and cute.

II. Though all of the boys
are allowed to make noise
I am told to exhibit politeness
and poise.

III. Nine times out of ten
I am listened to when
my ideas are echoed more loudly
by men.

IV. Chauffeuring my kid
I do just as I'm bid—
stay unseen, my opinions kept under
a lid.

V. I gum pureed fruit
and regret I can't shoot
all the nursing home staffers who murmur
I'm cute.

—Melissa Balmain

TO THE STARS AND BEYOND! WITH THE ELSON AUTO GROUP.

The clients of the Elston Auto Group—the finest luxury vehicle dealer in the Quad Counties area—have a passion for excellence. You demand the best from life. You will choose the extraordinary over the ordinary every time. That's how you've helped make the Elston Auto Group #1.

Now we have an offer for you that's out of this world!

Remember those times you watched the harvest moon rising over the fields, looking so big and clear you could almost touch it? Thanks to Elston Auto Group, now you can! Almost!

As a valued customer, you have the chance to write your name in the annals of space travel, as one of our lucky winners of a ride on our spacecraft, SpaceElston IV! It will be suborbital space, of course, and relatively short-lived, and you won't really be able to touch any-thing, but the view will be extraordinary.

And the prestige? Unbeatable! You thought your neighbors were impressed when you brought home your Jaguar XJ? Wait 'til you see their expressions when they see you on the local news in a white jumpsuit, returning after a successful (suborbital) space mission like a real American hero! Just visit us for a test drive to enter.

Our skilled technicians in the Research, Development & Service Bay have been working diligently on all the advanced technology needed—propulsion, aerodynamics, navigational interface, and of course weightless cupholders—to send two customers of Elston Auto Group plus pilot and technician into the wild blue yonder and the magnificent reaches of suborbital space! Every detail of the voyage will be exquisitely engineered and hand-crafted for your adventurous comfort. The imaginings of science fiction are now reality…for those elite customers who have the "right stuff" and come in for a test drive.

This entire program—which is now being copied by luxury vehicle specialists from Shanghai to Dubai—is the brainchild of our Special Events Director and #1 daughter, Kelly Elston. Even as a little girl, Kelly has been infatuated with the inky void of space. Even when poor math scores and a heart murmur kept NASA out of reach, she held onto that fascination. But in America dreams do come true, if you work hard enough and your family can fund the research.

Visit us for a test drive, and you'll be entered in the drawing for this once-in-a-lifetime dream opportunity. Your chances of winning increase every time you visit, or sign up for one of our personal wealth seminars, or attend one of our presentations on the exclusive resort lifestyle at Elston Del Mar, our new gated community near Guntersville, AL—less than an hour's drive from the Marshall Space Flight Center and Rocket Museum in Huntsville, where you can also get your interstellar "fix" on a regular basis.

And just for visiting, you'll receive a precision-engineered silver traveler mug modeled after the prototype containers on the space ship, emblazoned with the words "Future Member of the Elston Space and Auto Group" to remind you to look to the stars.

Visit us and test drive the latest new and certified pre-enjoyed models at the Elston Auto Group and enter to win. Along with Armstrong, Grissom, Jemison and Bezos, your name could be written in the stars! Suborbitally, of course.

—*James Finn Garner*

GOOD NAMES FOR YOUR PET DOG OR SNAKE.

Cooper, Bowser, Daisy, Scales (*snake only*), Rocky, Bailey, Dixie, Ginger, Death Coil (*snake only*), Bella, Max, Ye Legless Daemon (*snake only*), Temptor of Eve (*snake only*), Milo, I.B. Rattlin (*snake only*), Lulu.

—*Chris Galletta & Raven Burnett*

FAKE NEWS.

"Coffee Drinking Linked to Lower Mortality Risk, New Study Finds"-*NYT*

Alas, though the headline is earnestly meant,
our mortality risk's still 100 percent.

—*Melissa Balmain*

THE THIRD TORTOISE.

Tortoise One was slow but sure.
No breaks for him.
He plodded to the finish line and kept
   going.
Win or lose, he was who he was
   and so he would be forever.
The second, too, won a race against
   Achilles, the fastest of men.
While Achilles pondered how far he
   was going and how he could go at all,
Tortoise Two put one foot in front of
   another and another and another,
   caring nothing about the meaning
   of space or time.
Tortoise Three won no race.
An eagle picked him up, flew high,
   then dropped him on a rock to shatter
   his shell,
   to make him an easy meal.
But the rock was the bald head of an
   old man out for a walk.
The head cracked, but the shell did not.
Aeschylus, the tragic playwright, died
   in comic absurdity.
But the tortoise landed on his feet.
He was blessed and still is blessed.

No plodder he.
He had seen the world from on high,
   and a great man had died that he
   might live.
After twenty-five hundred years,
   he walks proudly,
   standing on the world,
   even if he can't understand it,
   and doing so at his own pace.

—*Richard Seltzer*

HOW TO POLICE A LAWFUL PROTEST.

What is a lawful protest?
Those are your typical free speech, anti-vax, or gun rights gatherings. Sure, sometimes neo-Nazis, white nationalists, and bigoted Christians show up, but it's our job as officers of the peace to protect their First Amendment rights.

What is an unlawful protest?
A group of radicals whining about police brutality, abortion rights, and racism.

A protest was just deemed unlawful. What happens next?
The protestors are now rioters. Your job now is to prevent further violence. Use any force necessary.

What if media personnel are mixed in with the protestors?
Assume everyone is a rioter and go from there.

What if a protestor gets hurt?
Who gives a fuck? They signed up for this.

What if an officer gets hurt?
Hunt the offender down and beat the ever-living shit out of them.

What if medics are providing medical support to injured protestors— should I assist them?
Are you some sort of pussy?

What if I'm afraid for my safety?
You will be afraid for your safety.

What if my kids ask how come they saw their father beat an elderly woman in the street?
You tell them, "Daddy was afraid for his life."

What if someone is using their voice in an aggressive manner?
You are a victim of assault. Fucking beat their ass.

How do I de-escalate a potentially violent situation?
I don't understand the question.

—*Julien Perez*

Tiny piano (with responsibly sourced keys!)

Custom Mosaic Artwork

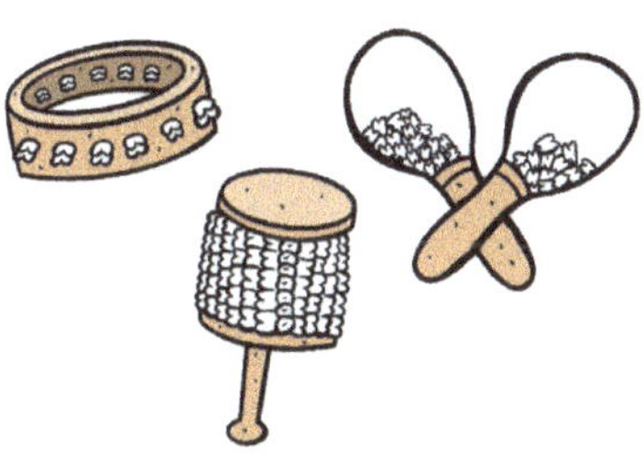

Assorted Hand Percussion Instruments (great for kids!)

Sequined Party Dress (only available in white, brush clean only)

Sack of Assorted Chompers

I TOOK A GENE TEST

by Nick Mullins

PITCHES I WAS ABLE TO SELL TO A STUDIO EXEC WHO IS A SHARK.

"Dude goes swimming with cut on foot"
The Seventh Seal
Injured Sea Lion I: The Reckoning
Shrinking Island
"Cruise ship capsizes—passengers are all obese and, get this: they have no weapons"
Air Is Water Now
Shark President
Shark Pope
Shark King
"*When Harry Met Sally* reboot, but this time between shark and severed human leg with still-pumping femoral artery"
"Like *Jackass*, but it's all sharks pranking orcas"
Operation C.H.U.M.
"It is 2049. Rain is sturgeon blood. It rains every day."
Injured Sea Lion II: "Blind, finless sea Lion wants to prove doctors wrong and go swimming"
Spring No Brakes!: "Bus full of college kids crashes into tanker truck of whale entrails, students decide to rinse themselves off in the open ocean"
Injured Sea Lion III: So Injured You Don't Even Have to Chew It
"*Eat, Pray, Love*, except instead of going to India she swims 50 yards into the ocean and thrashes seductively for an hour."
C.H.U.M. II: Stanky Tide
Huck Fin
　　—*Chris Galletta & Raven Burnett*

MY FAVORITE JOKES.

1. A doctor calls his patient and says, "I've got some good news and some bad news. Which do you want to hear first?"

The patient says, "The bad news."

There's a pause. The doctor says, "Usually, people want to hear the good news first."

"Well," says the patient, "You asked me what I wanted to hear first and I told you—the bad news."

There's another pause. "Can't we just try it again and you say 'the good news'?"

The patient changes doctors.

2. Two ants are walking along in the forest. One ant says to the other ant,

"We've been walking a long time and haven't found any food for the colony. Want to rest here for a while?"

"Sure," says the second ant. So they rest under a leaf. After a while, the first ant asks the second ant if he's ready to keep going. There's no answer. He asks again. Still, no answer.

Finally, he shakes the second ant, "Hey! I asked you if you wanted to keep going!"

"Sorry," says the second ant. "I must have dozed off." The first ant is completely disgusted. The second ant is surprised at the extremeness of the first ant's reaction. They keep walking. But there's tension.

3. Why did the chicken cross the road?

A butterfly flapped its wings in Mozambique.

Also, someone was chasing it, so it just ran like hell.

4. Two bars walk into a bar. One bar says to the other bar, "What are you doing in my bar?"

The other bar says, "Wait. Which bar asked me that? The bar I came in with, or the bar we walked into?" The other two bars are not amused. At all.

5. Yo mama is so fat, she has died. Because of her fatness.

6. If it's really true that blondes have more fun, then why do I often see brunettes having a lot of fun as well? Or is that just anecdotal?

7. An Amish man drives his buggy into town one day to trade some straw for a new toaster. On the way, his buggy breaks down. Two teenagers go zooming by in a Mustang convertible. As they whiz by, the Amish man shouts, "You got a toaster in that thing?"

8. A doctor, an engineer, and a lawyer go to heaven and are standing before the pearly gates. St. Peter calls the doctor forward and asks him gravely, "What did you do to help people when you were on Earth?"

The doctor says, "I was a surgeon. I operated on people and saved many lives."

St. Peter says, "Right, you're in." Then St. Peter calls the engineer and asks, "What did you do to help people when you were on Earth?"

The engineer replies, "I helped build bridges that allowed people to get to places they wanted to go."

So St. Peter says, "Right, you're in."

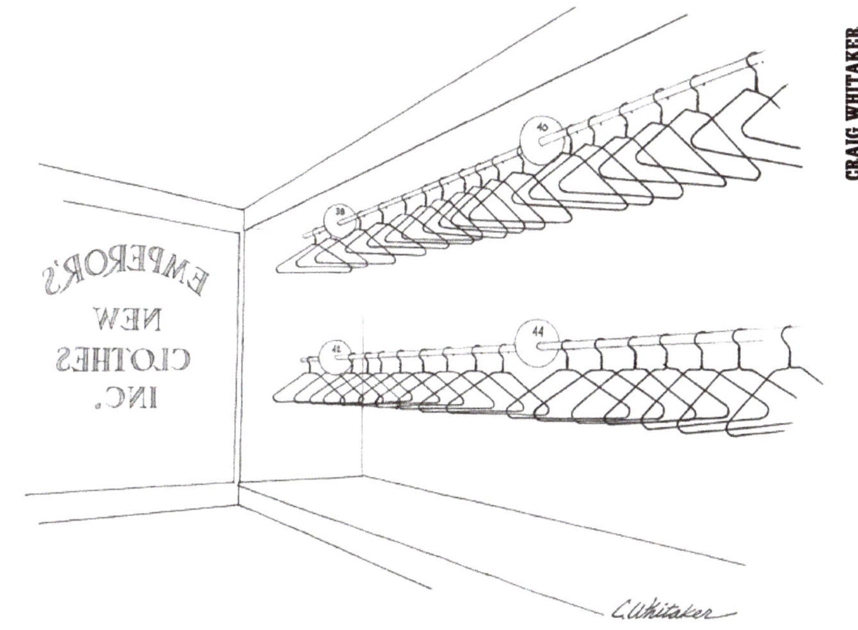

Finally, St. Peter calls the lawyer and asks, "What did you do to help people when you were on Earth?"

The lawyer says, "Very little."

St. Peter laughs and says, "Right, you're in."

Later, St. Peter realizes he has made a mistake. The doctor had been too ugly to be in heaven.

9. Adam is walking around in the Garden of Eden naked when suddenly he walks around a tree and sees God taking a leak. Adam says, "Wow. You're hung like a horse."

10. A woman goes into the confessional and says, "Forgive me, Father, for I have sinned."

The priest asks, "When was the last time you confessed, my child?" The woman takes a dump. Right there in the confessional.

11. A man walks into a confessional and says, "Forgive me, Father, for I have sinned. I told my wife to take a dump in the confessional. But honestly, I didn't think she'd do it."

"Whoa there, cowboy," says a voice next to him. "This is a public restroom."

"I thought it seemed like a crappy church," says the man, "but I didn't want to say anything."

12. A hunter shoots a duck and it plummets out of the sky. The hunter's dog goes running after it, roots around in the bushes for a while, and then finally comes back and lays the duck at the hunter's feet. But the duck was only winged and is still moving around. As the hunter is about to shoot the duck, it suddenly says, "Wait! Don't shoot!"

The hunter says, "Oh, my God! A talking duck!"

And then the duck says, "You're a sucky shot." The hunter can't believe it.

Then the dog says, "Yeah. You suck at hunting."

13. Knock, knock.

Who's there?

I'm not sure.

You're not sure?

No. I've been studying Buddhism.

Who was that, honey?

Some fucking Buddhist.

14. A redneck was visiting New York City for the first time. When he saw the Empire State Building, he couldn't believe how tall it was. As he stared up in wonder, a sophisticated-looking New Yorker walked by. The redneck turned to him and asked, "Excuse me, but do you know how tall that building is?"

The New Yorker replied, "Yes. But the number would be too high for a hillbilly to comprehend."

"Is it over a thousand?" asked the redneck.

"Yes," replied the man.

"Then you're probably right," said the redneck. "Still, it is beautiful."

The New Yorker paused, "Yes, I suppose it is. I guess I've never really appreciated it before." The redneck chuckled and shot him.

15. A bum walks up to a Jewish mother on the street and says, "Lady, I haven't eaten in three days."

The lady says, "You call that a problem? Let me tell you about prob-

"Listen, you knew I was a hobo when you married me."

lems. I've got problems! My son just dropped out of med school."

The bum looks at her, just stunned. *16*. A priest and a rabbi are in a bomb shelter waiting for the end of the world. Suddenly in walks a blonde, a lawyer, a doctor, a duck, a chicken, and a kangaroo. They all sit down. Then suddenly the earth shakes and the lights go off. The priest says, "Well, it looks like we're going to be here for a while. Does anyone know any good jokes?"

But no one does.

—Chris Spark

THREE STEPS TO A GREAT PAN SAUCE.

1. Make the pan sauce
2. Make it good
3. Make it great

—Chris Galletta

SCIENCE SAYS THIS IS THE RIGHT WAY FOR YOU TO BRING ME A WHOLE PIZZA IMMEDIATELY.

You've been bringing me a whole pizza immediately wrong for your entire life. It's natural to feel embarrassed about this, but help is on the way: Thanks to science, we now know how you can do it right. Here are the keys to success:

Bring me a good whole pizza. Don't cheap out. We live in New York City. I don't want Domino's. I will not accept Pizza Hut. Put in the time and money— bring me a pie from Lucali, as the experts advise.

Bring the whole pizza straight to me, without stopping anywhere else. Cold pizza is not as enjoyable as hot pizza, so make no stops en route from the pizzeria to my apartment. No, there's no exception for an "emergency." You will find that there isn't even a scientific definition of "emergency" in the first place.

Do not ask for money in exchange for the whole pizza. A truly kind gesture is one you offer with no expectation of anything in return. It's well documented that bringing this pizza to me is its own reward.

In fact, do not ask for anything in exchange for the whole pizza. Let me be clear: It's not just that I don't pay you cash for the pizza. I also don't owe you services, a favor…anything. The transaction is: You bring me the pizza. That's not me talking; it's the research.

Do not tamper with the whole pizza. I am direct; it's part of my personality, and it's a good quality. I refuse to waste your time by beating around the bush and pretending that I'm interested in matters other than getting the pizza in a prompt and proper fashion. But some people might grow to resent the type of straight shooter who tells them how to bring me a whole pizza. They could be tempted to eat a slice, spit on it, or make

**In Stores
August 2022
bobeckstein.com**

**"Picking the right
name for your cat
was never more
work—I mean fun."**

From the
award-winning
illustrator and
New York Times
best-selling author
Bob Eckstein

**"Totally unnecessary."
– *Neuters***

**Countryman
Press**

"On my Roomba's birthday I like to take him to the beach and just let him go nuts."

the little plastic table in the middle of the pie wobbly. Nope. Don't do those things. According to science, that is not how you are to treat the pizza you're bringing me immediately.

Do not ring my doorbell when you drop off the whole pizza. My dog barks when the doorbell rings, and I am already aware that you're bringing the pizza. Quietly leave it outside my door, and I'll go get it. Our knowledge of the physical world and its phenomena tells us that you can go back home after dropping off the pizza.

Do not forget the soda that goes with the whole pizza. This is common sense.

On second thought, maybe do ring the doorbell, then hang out and talk a little after you hand me the whole pizza. I've been lonely, and could use someone to chat with as I eat the whole pizza that you bring me immediately. What are your interests? Have you seen any okay movies lately? I may not enunciate the way you'd prefer, because my mouth will be full as I eat the whole pizza. Perhaps you'd like to play one of the 21 built-in games on my Super NES Classic Edition, if you brought your own controller (I don't want you to wear mine out). Remove your shoes before you enter. And don't take a slice of the pizza.
—*Jon Zeller*

THE POEM OF MINE THAT PEOPLE WILL SHARE WHEN I DIE.

It starts with trees and mulch. (Life's
   circle: noted!)
It doesn't dwell on government or guns,
so won't offend, no matter how you
voted.
It's free of puns.
Despite its morbid title, it feels breezy,
unlikely to depress you in the least.
It isn't sexy snark you'd be uneasy
   to show your priest.

This poem has no news or name
   checks in it,
no clues to decade, season, week or
   date—
which makes it timely if I die this
minute
or make you wait.

It barely mentions habits of ill breeding.
Its words are rarely of the vulgar sort.
And if you find it crap not worth
   rereading,
at least it's short.
—*Melissa Balmain* B

LET THE MATH GAMES BEGIN!

MORE THAN 70 COMPETITIVE CHALLENGES, PERFECT FOR GROUP OR SOLO PLAY

PERFECT FOR FAMILY GAME PLAY, OR SOLO CHALLENGES.

INCLUDES:

- ULTIMATE TIC-TAC-TOE
- SPROUTS
- BATTLESHIP
- QUANTUM GO FISH
- DOTS AND BOXES
- ORDER AND CHAOS
- SEQUENCIUM
- CATS AND DOGS
- *AND DOZENS MORE*

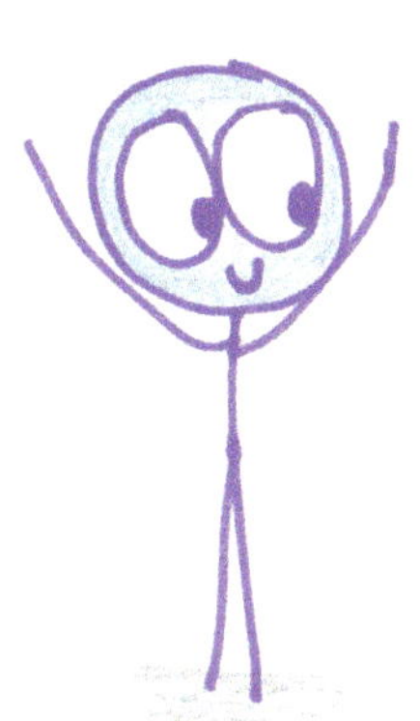

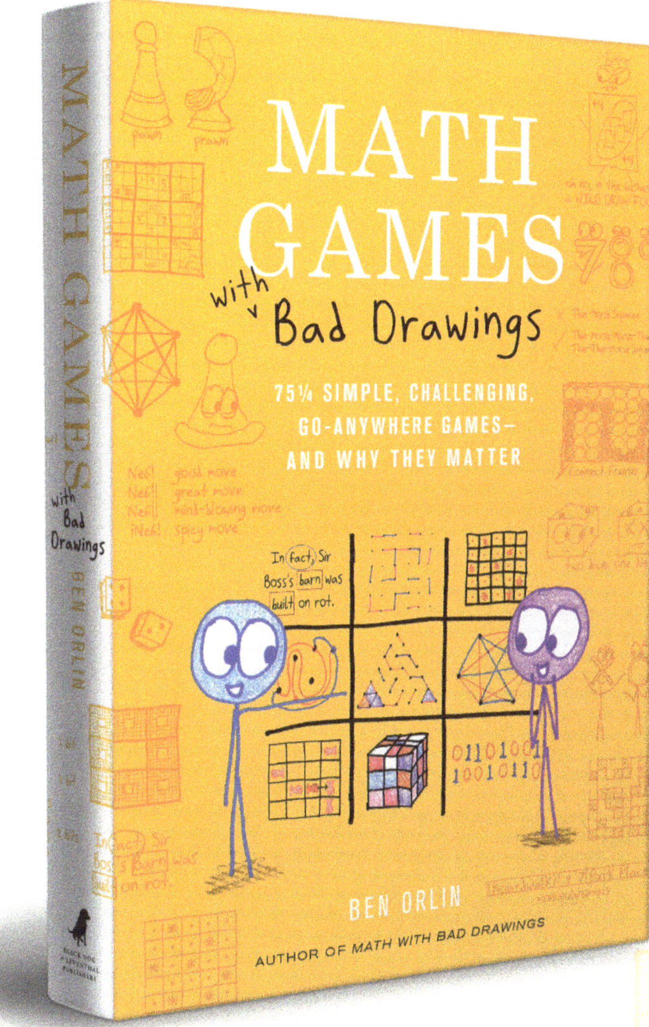

"I'm loving this math book with puzzles. Such a gentle, playful way to teach these abstract concepts. Like a pill pocket for math!"

— Allie Brosh, bestselling author of *Hyperbole and a Half*

A Fantastic, Frantic, Frenetic, Farcical Frolic of Full-on Foolishness Featuring the Fabled Foibles of the FABULOUS FURRY FREAK BROTHERS!*

* From FANTAGRAPHICS

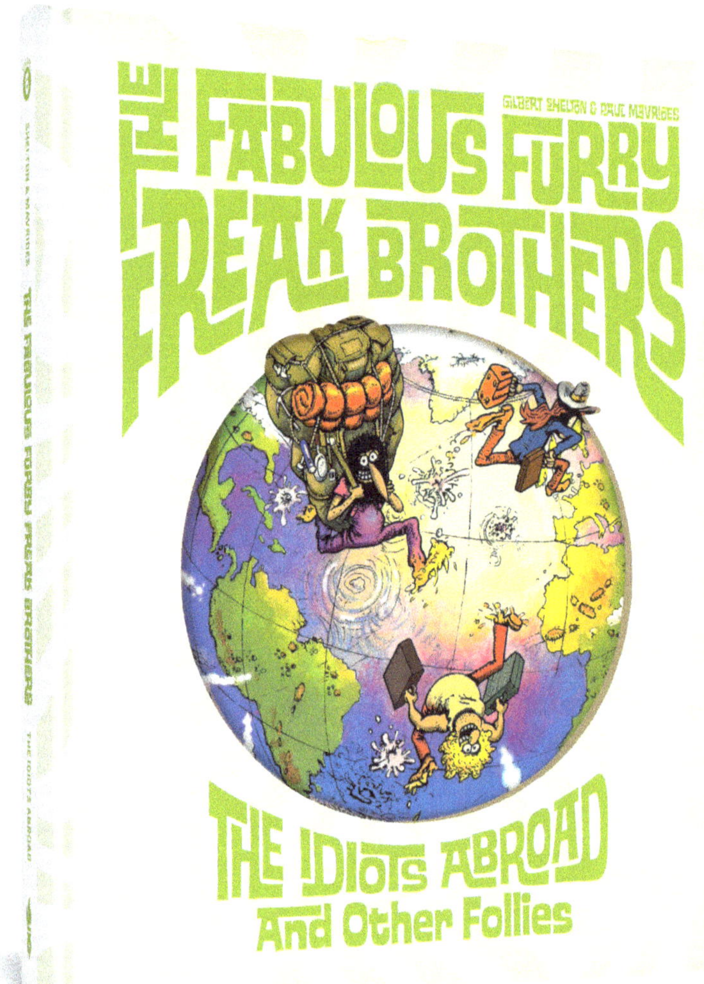

Phineas, **Freewheelin' Franklin**, and **Fat Freddy** head out with high hopes for Colombia, but (as always!) their plans go awry in the most hilariously self-destructive way possible. Scattered around the world — to Scotland, Russia, Africa, South America, and the Middle East — they manage to antagonize, offend, and otherwise annoy various groups of nuclear terrorists, human traffickers, pirates, and religious fanatics.

Meanwhile, **Fat Freddy's Cat**, abandoned at home, not only has his own adventure, he even sells the story to Hollywood!

Created in 1968 by Gilbert Shelton, The Fabulous Furry Freak Brothers are the world's most iconic underground comix characters, having sold over 45 million comics in 16 languages. The Freak Brothers' rollicking laugh-out-loud hijinks are comedic masterpieces overflowing with non-stop farce and satire.

✳ COMING SOON ✳

The Fabulous Furry Freak Brothers in the 21st Century

Freewheelin' Franklin, Phineas, and Fat Freddy form a band; bring home a stray container of plutonium; try to make it through a whole day without getting stoned; and help Phineas through his pregnancy.

The Fabulous Furry Freak Brothers: Grass Roots and Other Follies

The Brothers score some sinsemilla from a country cousin, start a softball league to score free drinks, adopt a possessed parakeet that outwits the D.E.A., and more!

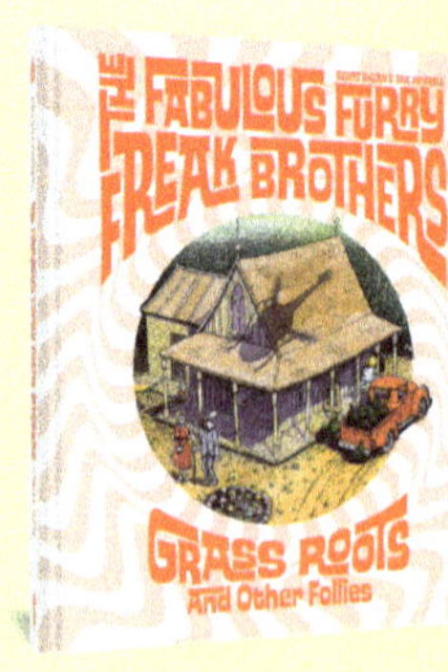

✳ www.fantagraphics.com/freakbros ✳

BY JEFF KULIK

TIDBITS!

Tidbits have seen you during bathroom time and wrote down everything they saw for purposes of blackmail.

'Tidbits! The modern taste sensation, straight from the farm to the dinner table. A versatile food product suitable for breakfast, lunch, or dinner. A powerful decongestant, gentle laxative, and shelf-stable gelatinous base for soups, stocks and stews. A veritable fiesta of sweetness and light, infused with enough umami goodness to power you through the next five days in a bare-knuckled blast of speed and pure energy. Tender enough to crumble into your chili, firm enough to add bite to your Salisbury steak. Tidbits are the future of hardcore gastronomical exploration.

Should you choose to take the plunge and enjoy Tidbits, they will quickly begin to transform your entire sense of being through a program of invasive gut-scrubbing and mellow meditative soul-plundering. Suitable for an elegant dinner party, yet in-your-face enough for your next confrontational theater happening, Tidbits will quite literally turn you inside out. Tidbits are already in your home.

Join in the fun and be born into everlasting life with the raw, surging power of Tidbits. In 12 oz., 72 oz., and Super-Hydrocephalic-Jumbo packaging for your next séance. Can be divided infinitely and never lose mass. Have been artificially aged in laboratory settings and shown to survive for thousands of years. Shelf-stable at temperatures up to 1000° Fahrenheit and as low as -750° Kelvin. Tidbits transcend the limitations of your puny, physical world.

After just five Tidbits, you will become one with Tidbits. Stop fighting and let the Tidbits wash over your thoughts, your memories, your being. Understand that Tidbits were you before you were you, but that you have never been and never will be Tidbits. You may experience a tingling sensation in your ribcage after eating Tidbits—don't worry, that's just Tidbits entering your Qi. Submit and allow them access; it will be well worth it.

If you discover any metal gears or brass components in your Tidbits, please contact **Mr. Don Weiss, P.O. Box 820, Hackensack, N.J. 07601**. Please include a detailed description of your find, as Mr. Weiss catalogs these for a very interested, very high-profile, yet very private fan of Tidbits in Great Neck, N.J. Should you wish to meet with Mr. Weiss, please let us know. He wants to know you, intimately.

While Tidbits can be used for routine canine dental care, they are not intended to be used as a glycol substitute in the manufacture of mass quantities of hand sanitizer. Please disregard all information circulating on social media to the contrary, as it was determined to have originated with the Ministry of Defense of the Democratic Republic of North Korea.

Every time you crunch a Tidbit, an angel gets its wings.

The Tidbits snacks originally referenced on that one episode of *Frasier* are not to be confused with the safe, reliable Tidbits currently on sale in the continental United States and the U.S. Marshall Islands. West of the Rockies, Tidbits are known as "Mountain Man Brand Lust Cakes" for reasons that are kept on file for review, by appointment, at the National Academy of Ultra-High-Frequency Broadcasting.

Tidbits were originally published under the name *Night of the Wombat*, and are once again legal to privately own in Tennessee. Tidbits are safe for war, children, and other living things. Please avoid direct eye contact with Tidbits. Clinical trials have demonstrated Tidbits as an effective treatment for hair loss. Do not use ceramic, glass, plastic, or paper plates for serving Tidbits. Tidbits exist outside of time and space.

Tidbits are the Alpha and the Omega. Resistant to rust, Tidbits made damn sure that Pilate washed his hands and sealed his fate. Tidbits have taken on forms that would seduce you into a frothy madness, yet are still gentle enough on your tummy that you can eat them before swimming. Tidbits understand that you're not like the others. Tidbits backwards is still Tidbits. If you were to hear Tidbits' real name, your consciousness would shatter. You would go insane.

Tidbits, from the makers of Le Petite Mort Gummies. A thrilling psychic experience through the darkest hidden recesses of the subconscious. Perfect for weddings, kids' birthday parties, rituals of all kinds and transubstantiations. Trust Tidbits, you'll thank them later.

JEFF KULIK *lives in Chicago with his wife and children. In addition to this magazine, Jeff has also been published in* Public Organization Review.

BY BEN ORLIN

WOE UNTO US, FOR WE HAD MIFFED THE GODS

One morning, the sky went dark and began to roll with syllables of thunder. THE WORLD SINS, spoke the thunder, AND MUST BE CLEANSED BY INCONVENIENCES.

"Why, gods, why?" we cried. "What have we done to deserve this?"

The gods did not reply. They merely continued: SEVEN INCONVENIENCES SHALL BEFALL THIS BLASPHEMING EARTH, AND THE FIRST SHALL BE…

We shuddered, waiting for Them to utter their curse. RECEIPTS.

We looked up in relief. Receipts? That didn't sound so bad. What was the risk—an avalanche of reimbursement? An excess of well-balanced checkbooks? It felt like the gods had really airballed this one.

But oh, They knew better than we.

Soon, receipts appeared unbidden in our purses and wallets. We found them piled atop our desks and wadded illegibly in the pockets of our laundered jeans. "When is this even from?" we would scream. "How did I spend $0.14 at a Honda dealership?" Soon we learned to fear proof of purchase in all its many guises. But the gods were far from done.

STILL THE WORLD SINS, the sky boomed. THERE SHALL COME ANOTHER INCONVENIENCE, MORE FEARSOME THAN THE LAST, AND IT SHALL BE…

We braced for doom. FORGETTING THY PASSWORD.

We seized on a glimmer of hope. Perhaps this burden would fall mostly on IT departments? With luck, might not the rest of us survive unscathed? Ah, we were fools. A blight upon the IT department is a blight upon us all.

First we lost email. Further password retrieval became impossible. We lost Amazon, Netflix, GrubHub. In our desperation, we created temporary accounts: overnight Facebooks, one-photo Instagrams, Twitter handles that muttered 280 characters into the abyss and then fell silent. We found ourselves lost in an infinite corridor of mirror-selves, each a distorted echo of the distorted echo that came before.

Oh, how we tried to remember those passwords. Mnemonics. Sticky notes. Each night in bed, I murmured my password over and over, and each morning I awoke with the bitter taste of adrenalin and shame. I spent days staring at my hands and arms, black with tattooed passwords, but never could I find the current one in the labyrinth of ink and errata.

We begged for mercy. The gods had no interest.

INADEQUATE ARMRESTS, cried the vengeful deities, and within hours, brother had turned against brother in a great passive-aggressive war for elbow space.

UNEVEN SIDEWALKS, cried the gods, and soon, desperate parents were navigating their strollers along the edges of the street, begging for death.

A BIT OF SUNSCREEN RUNNING DOWN YOUR FOREHEAD AND INTO YOUR EYES, they cried, and within moments it was like, oof, that kind of stings.

GROWN MEN IN BACKPACKS, cried the gods, and before anyone could quibble that this was less an "inconvenience" than an "annoyance," they were everywhere: adult men, thirty or even forty years old, with suits, mortgages, cufflinks, law degrees—and incongruous backpacks slung over their shoulders as if they honestly thought that was acceptable. Yet the gods were not done. Far, far from done.

STILL THE WORLD SINS, the thunder roared, AND SO THERE SHALL COME ONE FINAL INCONVENIENCE TO DOOM THE UNWORTHY…

As we waited, I heard sobs all up and down the street. PUNDITRY.

Wails of despair rose across the city. But it had already begun.

"The gods have issued a final inconvenience!" voices piped up. "But what does it mean? And where does this inconvenience rank on the list of other inconveniences? Tell us in the comments!"

"We've heard a million different inconveniences called the 'final' one," other voices chimed in. "That they keep recycling this tired line just shows their contempt for everyday citizens."

"This time is different!" screamed others. "This phenomenon is singular and unique. Do not look to the past. Do not reach for theory or framework. Make no effort to contextualize this event. Just lose yourself in the shrill melody of my dubious analysis."

No one knows why the gods grew vengeful again—and now, no one ever will.

B

BEN ORLIN *(@benorlin) is a math teacher and the author of three books, including* **Math With Bad Drawings***.*

BY K.A. POLZIN

EVERYBODY PLEASE MOVE ON TO SOMETHING ELSE

I admit it: the car accident was totally my fault. I forgot—that day was the day we switched sides, the day everyone in the country was meant to switch from driving on the left side of the road to the right. Despite the flyers, the billboards, the nightly announcements on TV, the talk in every store and café, still I got my rusted Honda started that morning and drove cluelessly for about two blocks on the left side of the road, ignoring the pedestrians waving their arms and yelling, unperturbed by the cyclist going the "wrong" way, until I rammed into Mrs. Roy making a right turn, with unfortunate results (which, again, were totally my fault).

Yes, I wish I'd figured it out right then and there, after crashing into Mrs. Roy (my fault), not persisted in my error, not shrieked at Mrs. Roy, pounded on her (now accordioned) hood, called her the regrettable names I called her (leave it at that), ignored the many frantic good samaritans who tried to intervene on Mrs. Roy's behalf but received only shoves and (in some cases) threats of violence from me and whom I called other regrettable names, wish I'd been a little quicker on the uptake, then perhaps everything that followed could've been avoided.

Because several people filmed the incident on their phones, and the footage was played on the nightly news, where I was rightly condemned, but I think they went too far, holding me up as an example of a poor citizen, the worst of the worst, wondering aloud how anyone could persist in such an error for so long despite having it carefully explained to them by multiple people, even police officers (when they finally arrived), calling my behavior "mind-boggling," even interviewing an old, embittered girlfriend (hardly objective), who confirmed my poor character and overall unworthiness.

But it turns out there were many wrong-side smashups that day, just as you'd suspect, though only mine made the news, and only because the others were quicker to comprehend their mistake, didn't raise quite the stink I did and, okay, didn't shove a crowd of people, causing some elderly folks to fall, and also some children (not on purpose!), but the point is they all made the same error. No one is perfect. I just ask for some understanding.

I do think the government should take some responsibility. Why did we switch sides nationwide, all in one day? It seems reckless. Could we not have had some kind of "soft open"? One county at a time, perhaps?

Yes I know, it was not the government who drove into Mrs. Roy, or who hurled scatalogical insults at the crowd, some of whom turned out to be nuns and schoolgirls. But no one was physically harmed! Mrs. Roy's front end has been repaired. What law, really, did I break (and don't say aggravated assault, because I never made contact with the tire iron)?

Okay, so my mother said *he's not the sharpest machete in the machete store*. But my mother should not be the final word on my character. This is my first offense, my first time threatening police officers, my first time brandishing a tire iron and shoving children and the elderly (and, I hope, my last). Mrs. Roy has even come to my defense, saying that to her knowledge I've never before behaved as frighteningly as this, that once I even helped her find her dog (I wish she had not added that I was twelve at the time).

I have been punished enough. I spent the night in jail. I was ridiculed by my cellmates (all perpetrators of real crimes). I must wear a disguise whenever I go out. My insurance did not cover the damage to my Honda. I found out my mother thinks I'm stupid.

So please: take me off the billboards. I look terrible in that photo, my face all furious and screamy, my arms mid-flail as I swing the tire iron, seeming every bit the madman. Stop using my name as a noun, as in "he really pulled an Edmund," or as a verb, as in "don't Edmund this up." And the memes: they are very hurtful. I never thought about the people in memes, how they felt, until I was featured in several hundred of them. Why, Nicki Minaj, do you keep sharing them? Do you not have music recording to do?

It's time to move on to something else. That man who married a chicken (sounds *genuinely* illegal). The triplets who weren't really triplets (all those lies they told!). The town that outlawed cats (are they onto something?). These are hilarious new topics. Whereas I am driving on the right side of the road now, with everyone else. I no longer own a tire iron (it's police evidence) or use my hands for shoving. I am too scared to yell.

Thank you for listening. Also, Mom, I'm told there's no such thing as a machete store.

B

PLOTKIN

BY MICHELLE HLUBINKA

WHITE HELLYPHANT

Yet another reason why never to go back to the office.

MICHELLE HLUBINKA

(Instagram: @hlubinka) is an illustrator and designer for MIT's Media Lab.

He was a Jewish kid from Brooklyn on his way to becoming the NFL's first great quarterback.

His father was the mobbed-up killer of his own brother-in-law, a murder that made headlines in New York City for years.

Sid Luckman would end up in the Pro Football Hall of Fame while his father became a secret he kept forever, even from his own children. **Until now.**

TOUGH LUCK

SID LUCKMAN, MURDER, INC., AND THE RISE OF THE MODERN NFL

by R.D. ROSEN

". . . a great and beautifully written untold story."—GAY TALESE

"A magnificent book."
—MARV LEVY, PRO FOOTBALL HALL OF FAME COACH

"Remarkable. . . . As compelling a book as I've read in a long time."—RICK KOGAN, CHICAGO TRIBUNE AND WGN RADIO

"With great research and storytelling, Rosen brings to life Depression-era New York and WWII-era Chicago in **a wonderful family saga that will captivate history and sports fan alike.**"
—PUBLISHERS WEEKLY

AVAILABLE AT ALL BOOKSELLERS

RDROSEN.COM

BY MICHAEL LODATO

CITIZEN OF JUDEA, CAN YOU HELP?

The midterms of 33 A.D. are the most important election of your lifetime."

Matthew, Can You Chip In to Help Unseat Pontius Pilate?
Matthew,

I know you get a lot of emails during election time, but this one you have to read.

It's no secret that Pontius Pilate has been a divisive dictator. Sometimes I feel like the only politician left who believes the Imperial governor should be about *bringing people together*.

That's why I'm running, Matthew—we need someone who will find common ground with the Empire. Unlike every other candidate, to me this ever-escalating Jesus situation is an opportunity for compromise.

The people want a moderate: I'm a tough-on-Jesus politician with a compassionate streak. My watershed "Seven Simple Edicts" (download the PDF here) aims to release Jesus in the next 10 to 20 years, while also instituting tough new penalties for future messiahs.

Matthew, it's time for real progress. Join our movement to free Jesus! (Eventually.)

CLICK HERE TO DONATE FIVE SHEKELS NOW

Mark, ANOTHER Pilate Gaffe
Mark,

The Imperial Governor is TERRIFIED of our campaign! That's why we're being attacked in the media and ambushed by camouflaged centurions we call "blasphemy actors." Pilate knows he's no match for our straight talk, so he has resorted to cheap tactics like arresting my campaign manager and torturing him to death. Is that what Judea is about? I say NO.

Hear me now, registered voter of Judea: I won't "wash my hands" of the important issues facing Romans, Jews, and Christians. And I'm not afraid to say it: Jesus makes some good points. The Romans have to bring down the temperature and quit flipping over the negotiating table.

The people need loaves *and* fishes! It's the right thing to do.
DONATE FIVE SHEKELS BEFORE IT'S TOO LATE

Luke, We Don't Need a Messiah. We Need Common Sense Solutions.
Luke,

Did you hear Pilate's latest attempt to smear our campaign?

He claims *I* support Jesus' signature policy: Loaves and fishes to feed 5,000. *That is a bald-faced lie.*

As I state clearly in the "Seven Simple Edicts" (download the PDF here) my Half-a-Loaf Plan provides *half-loaves* estimated to feed between 900 and 1,200 over the next two decades. Not miracles—just sound money management.

Policies like these have the support of the average Roman. Romans don't want their tax revenue going to feed the poor, and I get that. I believe your taxes should be used responsibly—for wars of conquest and tribute to Mars Ultor.

Support our common sense campaign!
GIVE FIVE SHEKELS NOW

John the Apostle, Let's Meet the Empire in the Middle
John,

I started this campaign because I knew I had the best ideas to improve this province. The Christians want to hand out loaves and fishes. Pilate and his Imperial flunkies want absolute power.

What happened to good old-fashioned COMPROMISE?

Some may try to divide us, but we've got history on our side. We all know that the pendulum swings far to the right and far to the left before settling in the center, right over the torso of my campaign manager (may he rest in peace).

Let's bring people together, not slice them apart!
WE NEED YOUR FIVE SHEKELS

Judas, We're Getting Killed Out There
Judas,

Did you hear the news from the herald? Pontius is so desperate he's offering 30 pieces of silver to anyone who turns over truthsayers like me.

Can you believe this, Judas?! The Emperor's silence on this is deafening.

Judea is divided, everybody knows that. In times like these, we need a unifier, Judas. As the only moderate in the race, I am not afraid to say what every Judean is thinking: both sides are to blame. What's Pilate going to do, crucify me?

Probably. But not if you
DONATE FIVE SHEKELS TODAY.

MICHAEL LODATO *(@magnesiummike) has written for* **Crash Course**, **McSweeney's**, *and* **Wisecrack**. *He once unknowingly offered an edible to a former Bush official, who declined.*

FOR THE LAW MAKER OR BREAKER IN YOUR LIFE.

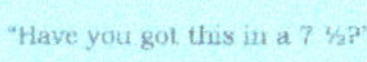

"He's an obvious flight risk, your honor."

"Don't you hate it when you plant evidence, but forget where?"

"Before we begin, I ask that you turn off all cell phones."

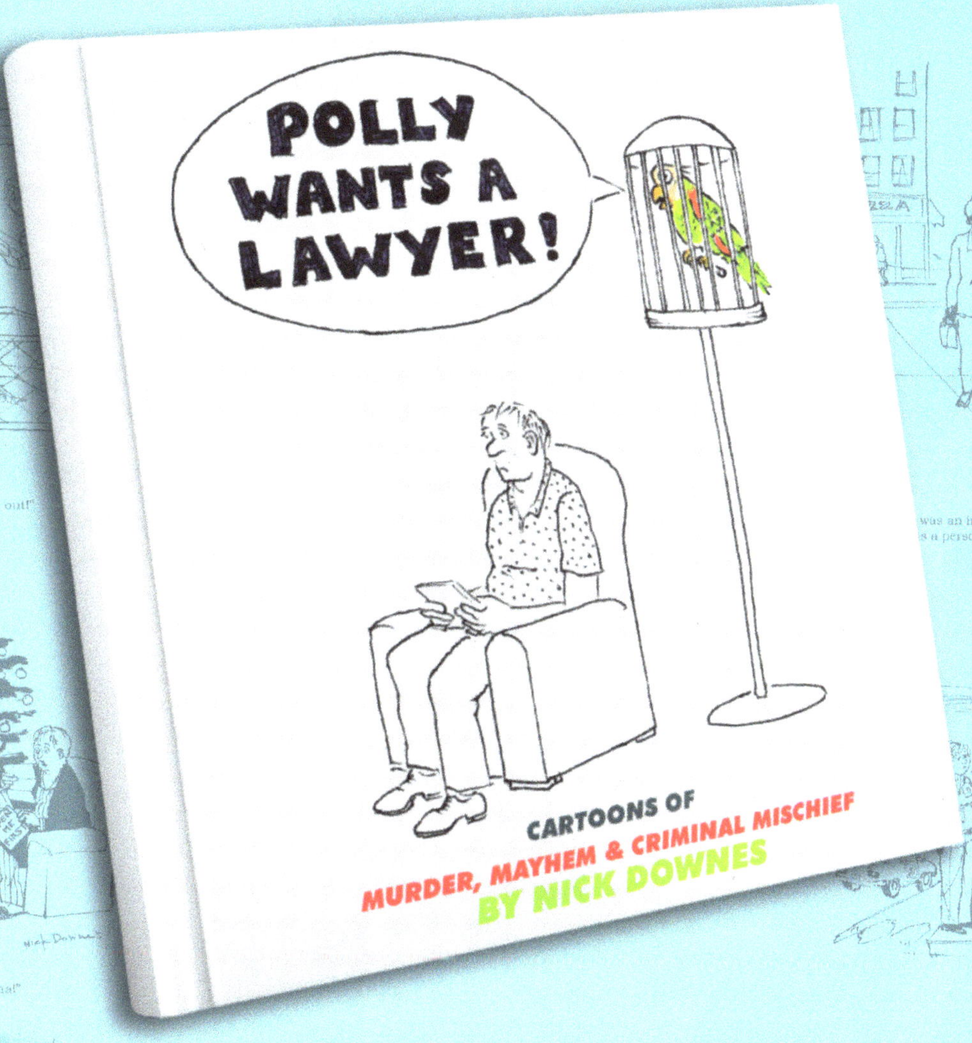

"He's tunneled out!"

"It's a subpoena!"

"Have you got this in a 7 ½?"

"Found him? But I've rented out his room!"

"In the venerable tradition of Charles Addams and Gahan Wilson, Nick Downes—with this collection of fabulously bizarre, twisted, and sometimes macabre gags—proves himself to be a cartoonist with a deliciously freaky sense of fun."

—Emma Allen, Cartoon Editor of *The New Yorker*

Humorist BOOKS

"★★★★★ Extraordinary."
— Youth Services Book Review

"Chwast's signature style is on full display...will induce giggles with each page-turn."
— Horn Book

"So much more than meets the eye...kids will love it!"
— Unleashing Readers

One of "the best new kids' books."
— Beyond the Bookends

"A clever way to encourage budding artists to look for visual correspondences in the world around them."
— School Library Journal

mineditionus
Astra Books for Young Readers

WHERE'S MY CAT?
SEYMOUR CHWAST

BRUSH WITH FAME?

3:30 TUESDAY AFTERNOON 1993

DAY DRINKING AND A BUCKET OF BALLS AT THE CORAL RIDGE GOLF COURSE IN NORTH FORT LAUDERDALE

COOL, THAT GUY ONLY HAS 5 BALLS LEFT..

HOLY SHIT! WHERE DO I KNOW THAT DUDE FROM?!

IS THAT RANDY WEST THE PORN GUY?!

IT TOOK ME A SECOND TO "SEE" WHAT I WAS LOOKING AT...

WHEN THE RANGE IS BUSY YOU WAIT BEHIND THE GUY WITH THE FEWEST BALLS LEFT TO HIT

DENIM

JUST THEN, HE TURNED TOWARD ME WITH ALL OF THE EASE AND CONFIDENCE OF A GUY WHO KNOWS YOU HAVE SEEN HIM HAVE SEX WITH SUPER HOT WOMEN ON CAMERA, FOR MONEY

THIS DUDE WAS IN A LOT OF PORNOS IN THE 80's AND EARLY 90's. A WHOLE LOT!

A SELECTION OF ACTUAL TITLES FROM THE RANDY WEST PORNO LIBRARY

LOAD WARRIOR

TRAMPIRE

RETURN TO BAZOOKA COUNTY

LOAD WARRIOR 2

THE ASSFORD WIVES

SNATCH BUCKLER

RANDY SMASHED HIS LAST FIVE BALLS AND NODDED AS HE ZIPPED THE COVER OVER HIS DRIVER, THE ONLY CLUB HE'D BROUGHT.

AS HE AND HIS DENIM AMBLED AWAY I HAD AN IDEA I SUDDELY COULD'NT STOP FROM TURNING INTO AN UNCOMFORTABLE REALITY...

I ALWAYS THOUGHT HIS WOODEN, REPETITIVE PRESENCE WAS KIND OF A BUMMER AND DIDNT ADD MUCH TO ANY SCENE

ROBOFOX

ROBOFOX II

WHO REAMED ROSIE RABBIT

HOWEVER, HIS COSTARS WERE ALWAYS TOP TIER HOT AND MORE THAN CAPABLE OF YANKING IN THE SLACK AND TAKING ON MORE THAN THEIR FAIR SHARE OF THE LOAD

Wednesday, April 17, 2019.

I stood in the doorway, blinking into the gloom. It was hopeless; the restaurant, a German joint on 22nd and Third, was dark and festooned with Christmas decorations. In that riot of fairy lights and *gemutlichkeit*, I could've peered inside for an hour.

"HEY SARGE!"

My head swiveled; after too many years of layout my peepers are *kaput*, but my ears are still pretty good. Like a *T. rex*; I point my head in the right direction and look for movement.

George was halfway back, his lanky frame folded into a booth. He and his lovely daughter Sarah were waving. I practically skipped to them.

For the three of us, if it wasn't love at first sight, that's only because we were talking on the phone. I should've known that any friend of Jack Ziegler's was a good egg, but I'd spent too many years marvelling at things signed "BOOTH" not to be nervous. It took George approximately thirty seconds to reassure me, and within five minutes, he'd demanded an assignment. "OK, Sarge, when do you need it?"

I laughed. I have an anarchic turn of mind, a chronically unmade bed, and a slight case of cerebral palsy—if you ever see me in uniform, we've lost. So George calling me "Sarge" was like me calling him "Tiny."

Back at Rolf's, George smiled. "So how are you, Sarge?"

"Let him catch his breath, Dad."

"I haven't slept for a week," I said, "but the magazine will survive another three issues. Possibly four."

"Good," George said. "We all need you."

"Not as much as I need all of you. What's good?" As I recall, we had *der schnitzel*.

Since George's death, many have written about the uniqueness of his humor, the antic elegance of his line, the magnificent clutter of his composition. All I can add is that to me, George Booth

was *The New Yorker*; whereas I could see Jack or Roz fitting quite happily into another magazine of the 1970s or '80s, there was something about George's work that sums up the pre-Tina *TNY*. His cartoons, and especially his covers, exuded a self-confident eccentricity that seemed to me, a Missouri boy, distinctly Yankee. Imagine my surprise when George told me that he, too, was from Missouri, the Western part even, where it's practically Kansas, which is practically Nebraska, which is practically the Dakotas. And here we both were in the

big city, fooling the New Yorkers. How long would that last?

The three of us ate and laughed, until LaGuardia beckoned. "When are you coming back out?" Sarah asked.

"Late fall," I said. "Or January. I always seem to come when it's coldest."

"Next time, you'll visit us in Brooklyn," she said. Sarah and I had bonded immediately. I tend to collect devoted sons and daughters, hoping they will rub off on narcissistic me.

"I'd like that," I said, and paid the bill. "Don't get up—"

George didn't listen. "Come back soon," he said with a hug.

"Just try and stop me," I said.

Then Covid hit, and that was the last time I saw George. But I see him still, towering, smiling. At ease, Marine, you've earned it.—**M.G.**   **B**

Burbank, We Have a Problem

The True Story of the Sixth (and Last) Faked Moon Landing

Editor's Note: This article was originally commissioned for the February 1973 issue of Playboy *but was cut to make room for their infamous "Girls of the Symbionese Liberation Army" photo spread and a 135-page "short" story by John Cheever. Reprinted without permission.*

Lunar Module Pilot Cleve Sharp is in trouble. The view from his tiny space capsule, though obscured by the fog of his own rapidly accelerating breath, tells the whole story. The Naval aviator and aeronautical engineer's bright blue eyes see what his brain cannot yet process.

It's Carol Burnett.

"Cut! Back to one, everybody! Ms. Burnett, you're on stage 12 this week. And this is a closed set."

"Closed set my knee. You snow snorters are faking a moon landing."

"No, we're not!" yells director Stu Washington. "Not at this rate, at least."

As the whole world knows by now, the original moon landing was NASA's biggest success since Tang. Directed by Stanley Kubrick and starring Neil Armstrong, Michael Collins, and Buzz Aldrin, *Apollo 11* nabbed the second highest TV ratings of 1969, just behind Tiny Tim's wedding on *The Tonight Show* and just ahead of Tiny Tim's divorce on *The Dick Cavett Show*.

"The picture was fantastic, but Stanley's a miserable son of a bitch," explains Apollo producer Syd "the Kid" Meyerowitz as we sip grasshoppers while driving down Mullholland. The Kid, 87, pilots his Rolls Royce with the same abandon he brings to his hit films like *Groovy Police*, *Hippies in Space*, and *The Sorrow and the Pity*. "I call him and say, 'Stanley, babe, we're doing boffo numbers, and the boys in Cape Canaveral want you back.' And you know what he tells me? He says, 'I don't do sequels.'

"Which, come to think of it, is the same thing he told me when I pitched him *Spartacus 2*."

However, as the saying goes, the show must go on. Within hours of his conversation with Kubrick, Meyerowitz had signed Orson Welles to take over the franchise.

"I knew Orson would say yes. He was pretty deep in debt. He'd run up a tab at the Hamburger Hamlet near Paramount —it was something like $60,000, which was crazy because he'd only been there three or four times."

However, despite his genius, Welles proved to be a difficult collaborator. "He spent the first three hours on set telling the story of the time he got 'manual pleasure' from Eva Braun," explains Meyerowitz as he pulls his car over to check the damage he had just inflicted on a school bus. "In his defense, the handie itself took eight hours. Apparently, she was terrible at it."

Eccentricities aside, Welles still delivered a well-received, if workmanlike, second installment in the series. However, when he got to *Apollo 13*, things took a turn for the worse.

"I get to set, and Orson tells me that he brought Bill Goldman in for a rewrite. Bill has this *fakakta* idea that 'it would be more exciting if they don't get to the moon.' What kind of *schmegegge* is that? That's like saying that it's more fun to go to Ciro's when Liz Taylor's in rehab."

Meyerowitz throws his hands in the air. He's clearly still upset with how *Apollo 13* went. Nevertheless, the producer has a job to do, so he hands a cop a $200 bribe, signs an autograph for the ambulance driver, pours himself another grasshopper, and gets back into his Rolls.

"We had trouble finding good directors from then on," Meyerowitz laments as his car tumbles down a canyon a few hundred feet past Coldwater. "NASA wouldn't approve anybody. Bergman? Too European. Mel Brooks? Too Jewish. Clint Eastwood? Not Jewish enough."

Meyerowitz rolls his eyes. We both know where this conversation is going. "That's how we got Stu. Now, will you help me get my Rolls out of this pool? I know it's a rental, but I don't want to be a schmuck."

Stu Washington is a beaten man. Literally. Carol Burnett just kicked his ass.

"She jumped me. Came out of nowhere. I asked her, 'Why are you hitting me with a klieg light?' She told me it was a 2K blonde. She knows her stuff. Total pro."

☛

❖

Stu knows a thing or two about being a pro. Barely 24 years old with over 4,000 directing credits to his name, Stu is the man that studios call when the job has to get done fast.

"I've directed at least 100 episodes of *Gunsmoke* and 75 *Flip Wilson Shows*. "I once directed *Mary Tyler Moore* and *Kojak* at the same time. Gavin MacLeod did a great job as a dead hooker in both."

Stu is a new generation of director. Eschewing the auteur posture of contemporaries like Francis Coppola and Peter Bogdanovich, Stu prefers a more collaborative, schedule-driven approach.

"I tell everybody the faster we get the shot, the sooner we can go to the orgy at Warren Beatty's house." Then he cracks a wicked smile. "And if that doesn't work, I tell them my uncle is Lew Wasserman."

"Uncle Lew" was instrumental in getting Stu his moon landing gig. "Was-serman shoved him down my throat," explains Meyerowitz. "That's normally something he only does at Warren Beatty's house."

Stu, who changed his name from Wasserman to Washington while trying to bed a Roosevelt at Choate, believes that his moon landings are the best ones yet.

"It wasn't until *Apollo 14* that people played golf on the moon. That was my idea, you know. I got it while playing golf."

With the addition of the Lunar Rover in *Apollo 15* and *Apollo 16*, Stu feels he's found his stride. "I had just directed two episodes of *Streets of San Francisco* over my lunch break, and I knew I had to bring that energy to the moon."

Unfortunately, Meyerowitz is less optimistic about *Apollo 17*, which, if it bombs, could be his last. "Four years, that's a good run. The first one's the one they all talk about, anyway. And NASA's got a new Head of Programming—"

"Her actual words were, 'Give us *Deep Throat* in space,'" interjects Stu. "I've already asked wardrobe to mock up some crotchless spacesuits."

"We'll also need to cast some women."

"Is Nancy Reagan available?"

"Ron nixed it. Says space is Jerry Brown's thing." Meyerowitz's expression is of a man of a man who's been through it all many times before. "They told me if we don't win our time slot, the moon is canceled," he shrugs as he eats a bowl of Quaaludes like breakfast cereal.

"Impossible. This is the best one yet," replies Stu, sipping bourbon and penicillin, a cocktail he calls "Shirley MacLaine's Revenge."

"Oh yeah?" replies Meyerowitz. "What are we up against?"

Stu checks that morning's *Los Angeles Examiner* for the TV listings. "Uh-oh. Looks like Tiny Tim is having a child custody hearing on *Laugh-In*."

Meyerowitz swallows his Quaaludes and groans. "We're screwed." **B**

"From the depths of my mother's basement, I stab at thee!!!"

"Well, well—if it isn't Jimmy 'The Flusher' Flynn.
And all grown up…"

"Maybe we just leave this part out."

Nick Spooner
is a commercial film director
who dreams of becoming
a full-time cartoonist.

HERMETTE WIRELESS

Don't call us and we won't call you.

It never needs charging!

Always be out of reach!

Blame the crappy service at Hermette Wireless!

"I save hundreds of dollars on data! Just...wow!"
     -Ira M.

"My kids were always staring at their phones. Now they stare at me! Thanks!"
     -Jackie L.

"I maximized my hermit life-style. It literally doesn't work anywhere!"
     -Laurie R.

"World's best burner phone. Perfect for camping!"
     -Susan H.

The leave-me-alone wooden phone!

Get the latest phone from Hermette Wireless... a phone-shaped hunk of wood that gets zero reception no matter where you are. Our phones are handmade of solid reclaimed wood. Each one is different and none of them work. Your phone does not get Twitter, Facebook, Instagram or Parler. You won't get texts, calls or emails. No meditation apps. No productivity apps. No apps at all. No podcasts. No maps. No games. No camera. Nothing. Perfect for curmudgeonly seniors. Tweens love it too! Simple to use. You just carry it around and stroke it to calm yourself down. Stop doomscrolling and start self-soothing with the hardwood quality that comes from Hermette.

Don't follow us.
@hermettewireless

Carnal Knowledge

"In order to protect his chastity, it is recorded of him that he never once looked straight at any women."
—Fr. John A. Hardon, S.J.,
Life of St Aloysius Gonzaga, *2000.*

First thing one October Monday, Mr. Mc-Quillan informed me that I was excused from class and summoned to the office of Father Noble. The scuttlebutt was that it was Father Noble's job to introduce us first-year pupils to the Facts of Life.

Edward Noble, S.J. was impossibly old. He had a parchment-white complexion, sunken cheeks, chalky teeth too big for his gaunt face, and wore rimless specs. We called him, for obvious reasons, "Dead Ed." His office was adjacent to forbidden territory, the college library. (Father Noble was also the college librarian, who allegedly withheld from his customers every book on the *Index Librorum Prohibitorum.*)

His door was open. Father Noble stood and welcomed me with a well-practiced rictus smile, pointed me to a chair, and sat gingerly back down behind his unnecessarily large desk.

The author a few years after the incident in question, having discovered he preferred drama to Sabrejets.

At my age, the cleric observed, I must be curious about sex. Hmmm? Just what, he asked mildly, did I already know?

I was a 13-year-old Irish Catholic lad. I had a sketchy idea of where babies are hatched (because "blessed is the fruit of thy womb") and I had heard theories about how couples put one in there. The previous August, my cousins and I had huddled to pool our misinformation. We agreed that a bush and a cherry were involved somehow. And pussies and cream. There were clearly a lot of details, which remained murky. My main thought was simply this: you'd have to want a baby an awful lot to go to all that embarrassing trouble.

While my knowledge of sex (and nearly everything else) was limited, one thing I did know about was fighter planes. I had, for the last few years, been extremely fond of comic books, particularly "war-in-the-air" comic books. I filled many notebooks with sketches of the blue Korean sky filled with silver Sabrejets in red-hot combat with silver Russian MIGs. Sabrejets, I knew, had broken the sound barrier. Sabrejets were (allegedly) made in Canada. My prepubescent crush on the Saberjet had inspired me to join the Royal Canadian Air Cadets. Every Tuesday parade night forty of us, ages 12 to 18, drilled in a vast public high school gym. "Squad will march in column of route, by the left, quick, *march!*"

Boring, yes. But I did get to wear a scratchy blue-gray battle dress uniform and wedge cap. I learned how to salute an officer—longest way up shortest way down—and always to call the Toronto airport "Air Defense Command."

One memorable Saturday a bunch of us were bussed out to Air Transport Command (Montreal airport) and loaded onto a DC-5M transport, the plane that gloried in the name of "North Star." Our short flight was oppressively hot, unbearably noisy and painfully unpressurized. Heaven.

Occasionally, after much marching, we cadets attended the screening of an official, black and white, scratchy, RCAF training film, *e.g.*, how to signal to the pilot that the chocks are out from under the wheels. And once—possibly by accident—

Canadian writer and parodist **Sean Kelly** *transmuted his Irish Catholic boyhood into laughter via books like* **How to Be Irish** *and* **Saints Preserve Us!**. *This piece is excerpted from Sean's long-threatened memoir,* **The Boy Saints**.

we were treated to a vividly graphic, black-and-white, WWII-era cautionary documentary about the consequences of contracting syphilis. The sight of so many riddled, ravaged (and astonishingly large) penises was—in the words of a then-popular song—unforgettable.

So when "Dead Ed" got around to the subject of venereal disease, I was way ahead. My casual description of the wrecked penises I had seen on-screen sent the kindly old librarian off-script and into a huff. After all, it was *his* job to enforce my fear of sex, but clearly the R.C.A.F. had beaten him to it.

Determined to reassert his authority, Father Noble demanded that I immediately quit "that wretched Protestant paramilitary organization," and was gratified to learn that I had already done so, (without seeing a single Sabre Jet). The rest of our interview was awkward; since "Dead Ed" had perhaps a limited amount of personal experience to draw upon, he was unable to do much improvising. One of the things we didn't talk about at home was what people did or might do with their pants off; here with Father Noble, I made a mental note to be likewise discreet when the topic arose in the presence of clergy.

Still determined to give me a good shot of sex-fear, Father Noble dismissed me in time for lunch—but not before introducing me to the possibility of masturbation.

As boarders at Xavier, we were obliged to attend Mass every morning and expected, when summoned by bells, to rise from the pew, proceed to the altar rail and kneel, then have the host laid on our tongues by a mumbling priest; that is, to receive Holy Communion. If you remained in your pew, it was understood that you were ineligible to partake in the sacrament because you were not in a State of Grace, but rather in a State of Mortal Sin. This was humiliating, since the only Mortal Sin to which we had the slightest access was "self-abuse."

Every morning, one or two Jesuit priests were on duty in the confessionals at the back of the chapel, and they were kept busy. These poor souls were obliged to hear whatever euphemism for jerking off you preferred, to remind you that your body is a temple of the Holy Ghost, and then to grant you absolution—thereby returning you to a State of Grace, fit once more to ingest the Body, Blood, Soul, and Divinity of Jesus Christ. They knew you'd be back tomorrow. They had the worst job in the world. **B**

"Let's put another doohickey on the bottom."

HOW
SIX
MADE
GOOD
IN THE WORLD

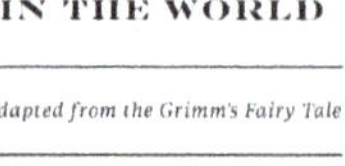

Adapted from the Grimm's Fairy Tale
BY SHAWN CHENG

Once there was a man who fought in the King's war with hopes of fame and fortune...
The King thanks you for your service.
Three farthings?

Tuh!
I shan't forget this injustice.

Golly!

My, you're strong!
Why don't you be my servant?
Ok

Together we two shall make good in the world!

Pow!

Ahem..
I'm afraid you've missed your mark, huntsman.
Eh?

I beg your pardon, sir.
But I was aiming for the fly on its back.
Its left eye, actually.

Amazing!
Why don't you be my servant?
Ok

Together we three shall make good in the world!
Strange... No breeze stirs, yet those windmills turn as if driven by a raging tempest!

Ahoy, neighbor!
Why do you exert yourself in this manner?

In yonder field there are seven windmills. I am making them turn to pass the time.

Fantastic!
Why don't you be my servant?
Ok

Together we four shall make good in the world!

Here is another strange sight...
Ahoy! You seem to be in quite an uncomfortable state of affairs, friend.
Hm?

You see, sir, my legs churn like the wind.
I would tire myself out if I wear them all the time.

Incredible!
Why don't you be my servant?
Ok

Together we five shall make good in

Why, sirrah, do you put your cap on properly?
You look quite ridiculous.
Um

I assure you, sir, this is a necessary arrangement...
For if I set my cap straight, a terrible frost engulfs me and my surroundings.

...
Well, I suppose you should come with me.
Ok!

What's this?
The King has proclaimed that whosoever wins a foot race with his daughter shall be her husband.
This is it, gentlemen...

Together we six shall make good in the world!

O King, I have come to challenge your daughter for her hand in marriage.
I only ask that my servant runs in my place.

Very well. And if he loses, you shall both lose your heads.
Do you accept these terms?

In fact, your majesty, we six shall all stake our lives on the outcome.
Oh ho ho ha! I like your style!
...

Beyond the dunes lies an oasis.
The first to return with water from that spring shall be the winner.
Hmph!

Come, show us how nimble these legs are.

Begin!
oh!

Indeed, she is quick. But I can outrun the wind itself!

!!

Just like that, he's gone!
Don't worry, I shall keep him in my sights.

He has already reached the spring and filled up the water jug.
Now he's returning — he's just passed the princess going the other way!

Boy, this is much too easy.

Let me take a short break...
Whew.

z z
z

...
z z

Impudent knave!

Ho ho! What a turn of events!
Looks like the princess now has a decisive advantage!

Take heart, gentlemen.
I shall rouse our comrade from his foolish complacency.

POW!
EEP!

Egads!

O foolish
fool!

Don't fail me now, my legs!

Here she comes!
Summon the Executioner!
Oh!
Not so fast! Look!

!
Here he comes!

Strike the wedding bells, Your Majesty!
We shall soon be united as in-laws!
Indeed...

Fear not, my daughter...
I will not allow you to marry this common soldier.
BOO HOO HOO
You called, My Liege?

Please make merry amongst yourselves in our "Iron Hall"!
The banquet will begin shortly.

A toast, gentlemen. To making good!
Hear, hear!
To us six!
I do hope the feast begins soon...

It won't be long...
I smell a great fire burning.

Whew!
It is getting warm in here.
I'll crack open the door.

Zounds!
We're surrounded by flames!!

Foul, foul treachery!
Oh!
It's a trap!
Woe!
All's lost!
Do not despair, my friends!

Gather around me!
I shall summon a blanket of cold to save us from the flames.

If any still live, we shall behead him.
Ho ho!

Brrrr...
Treacherous tyrant!

G-G-Gold! I can pay you gold!
But please... spare my daughter... and leave in peace...
Very well...

Take only what you can carry from the treasury...
Then begone!
As you wish, Your Majesty.

Let me take care of this.
My thoughts exactly!

Sire! The Treasury...
Peace, man! I had to pay off those vagabonds.
Now, how much did they take?

...
Um... They took everything, Sire...
I-Impossible!!

I don't think this is what the King had in mind!
Ha ha!

After them!!

We're being pursued.
I shall deliver the final blow!

HFFFF...

WOW!

Well, gentlemen...

We made it!
FIN

Hauge's 2022 in Review

Consider this your trigger warning.

Follow Ron as he makes Instagram safe for satire, one cartoon at a time: @ron_hauge.

Young Trump
IF YOU COULD TRAVEL BACK IN TIME AND WARN HITLER, WOULD YOU DO IT?

The Meth Gala
HAUGE
MAG
NO VAXEEN

The American Experiment
HAUGE

HAUGE
Ceci n'est pas un crime.

Republican Earth Day
HAUGE
EQUAL JUSTICE IS AN ILLUSION
HAUGE
Greetings FROM
FLORIDA
HAUGE
TILL GAY AS FUCK!
DECLASSIFIER
USES HIS MIND
TOTAL BULL·SHIT
NOT SECRET
SECRET
TOP SECRET
HAUGE

HAUGE
PEE TAPE 1
PEE TAPE 2
PEE TAPE 3
PEE TAPE 4
PEE TAPE 5
PEE TAPE 6
PEE TAPE 7
PEE TAPE 8
PEE TAPE 9
PEE TAPE 10
PEE TAPE 11
PEE TAPE 12
PEE TAPE 13
PEE TAPE 14
PEE TAPE 15
PEE TAPE 16
PEE TAPE 17
PEE TAPE 18
PEE TAPE 19
PEE TAPE 20
PEE TAPE 21
PEE TAPE 22
PEE TAPE 23
PEE TAPE 24
PEE TAPE 73
PEE TAPE 74
PEE TAPE 75
PEE TAPE 76
PEE TAPE 77
PEE TAPE 78
PEE TAPE 79
PEE TAPE 80
PEE TAPE 81
PEE TAPE 82
PEE TAPE 83
PEE TAPE 84
PEE TAPE 85
PEE TAPE 86
PEE TAPE 87
PEE TAPE 88
PEE TAPE 89
PEE TAPE 90
PEE TAPE 91
PEE TAPE 92
PEE TAPE 93
PEE TAPE 94
PEE TAPE 95
PEE TAPE 96
PEE TAPE 145
PEE TAPE 146
PEE TAPE 147
PEE TAPE 148
PEE TAPE 149
PEE TAPE 150
PEE TAPE 151
PEE TAPE 152
PEE TAPE 153
PEE TAPE 154
PEE TAPE 155
PEE TAPE 156
PEE TAPE 157
PEE TAPE 158
PEE TAPE 159
PEE TAPE 160
PEE TAPE 161
PEE TAPE 162
PEE TAPE 163
PEE TAPE 164
PEE TAPE 165
PEE TAPE 166
PEE TAPE 167
PEE TAPE 168

Rudy Fails To Pass The Ba
COCK
HAUGE

HAUGE
Birth
Control

ADOPTION CLINIC
HAUGE

Bedminster
3 HOLE 3 3
FUTURE HOME OF
Melania Trump
HAUGE

Trump In Disappointing Halloween Candy
HAUGE
WELCOME GREAT PUTIN
HAUGE
GOTHAM VOTES TOD...
POLLING PLACE
HAUGE
819016
Max The Vax Says:
I SWEAR TO GOD, YOU SENSELESS ANTI-VAX SCUMBAGS, I WILL HAUNT YOU IN YOUR FUCKING CASKETS. GET YOUR GODDAMNED SHOTS. HOLY CHRIST.
HAUGE

Santa Claus Is Coming to Town

(With a devil and a whipping stick.)

I think we can all agree that children are appalling creatures. They are prone to habitual sociopathy year-round, but they seem to worsen during the holiday season. They instinctively sense an adult's seasonal obligation to indulge them, and the merest whiff of tinsel is like catnip to a rabid, feral stray. To curb this unbridled narcissism, the invention of Santa Claus's good/bad list was vital; indispensable for distressed adults burdened with the onerous task of overseeing their offspring's development.

Case in point: When I was eleven years old in the early 1980s, my best friend received a calculator for Christmas. Far from being a rudimentary arithmetic instrument, it was one of those scientific calculators with innumerable keys depicting arcane mathematical symbols which offer exhaustive, but typically unexplored, mathematical functionality. We all received these "grown up" calculators at this juncture in our lives from optimistic but delusional parents who hoped in vain that we'd go on to excel in high school. This, despite the fact that my school was, and always had been, little more than a factory line which supplied new recruits to the retail, car repair, and metalwork industries, not to mention the expanding unemployment lines. Suffice it to say that giving a scientific calculator to my friend, myself, or any of my peers, was akin to putting a mango in charge of the International Space Station with the hope that it will somehow navigate its way to Jupiter and back.

Anyway, my friend received this calculator and his parents proudly observed that, during the lagging week between Christmas and New Year, their son eschewed the more juvenile of his gifts—the toys and games—in favour of his new electronic device. He also spent hours methodically entering neat lists of numbers in his new notepad with his new fountain pen. His parents perceived this as a sign that their son was on his way to becoming a man, and had put away childish things, such as the belief in Santa Claus and his crudely moralizing Lists.

Finally, a few days later, my friend invited his parents to take seats at the kitchen table as if interviewing them for a job. He explained his week's labour to them as meticulously as he could, pointing to the relevant entries in his notepad. He'd researched every gift he had received from them and written down all the details: the shop from which each gift had been purchased and how much it had cost. And then, in another set of neatly pencilled columns, he had entered the cost of every gift his sister had received. After delivering these figures and his working methods, he ceremoniously presented his bemused parents with a piece of paper, which he had neatly torn from the notepad and folded for the sake of polite discretion.

Opening the paper, as if it were the announcement of an Oscar winner, his parents read the following:

"This Christmas you spent £106.77 on presents for me. However, you spent £120.45 on my sister. This means that there is a deficit of £13.69 (If you don't believe me, you can borrow my calculator). How would you like to balance this shortfall? Cash is preferable, though cheque, postal order, or gift voucher are also acceptable."

My friend's parents instantly resented their son's newfound ruthless maturity. Incensed, his affronted father blurted out that his son was deeply ungrateful and had, only a matter of days after Christmas, already made Santa's Naughty List. But my friend sneered at the notion—he was now too old to believe in such infantile nonsense.

When, by chance, my friend slipped on ice the next day and broke his calculator, as well as two of the fingers that were holding it, his father remarked, "Wow, Santa works fast. Never mind the naughty list: Looks like he has a hit list, too."

············ ◆ ············

Richard Littler *is the creator of Scarfolk. Scarfolk is like…if George Orwell wrote for* **The Onion**? *That doesn't do it justice. Anyway, Richard lives in Switzerland.*

*"I'd much rather see them swimming free
and not caged up like that."*

The "List" is alluded to in the lyrics of the seasonal favourite "Santa Claus is Coming to Town":

*He's gonna find out
Who's naughty or nice…
He sees you when you're sleeping,
He knows when you're awake,
He knows if you've been bad or good,
so be good for goodness sake*

But this system of implied penalization for misconduct is just that: implied. All said and done, the intention of the list is merely to gently intimidate kids into behaving a little more altruistically; there isn't really a "Naughty List," no formalised policy of systematic punishment…

Or is there? One dark December evening I learned, with a modicum of horror, that other cultures fervently put the concept of "The List" into practice. I found myself snowed in in a remote mountain village in the Bavarian Alps. The trip hadn't been intentional; I didn't know anyone there; I didn't speak the language. Only a couple of hours before, I had been enjoying "a quick drink" after work with German colleagues in a busy city bar during a brief business trip to civilized Munich. One minute I was politely eating Weißwurst, downing beer and Williams schnapps—my colleagues had wanted to introduce me to local culture—and the next I was alone on an empty regional train heading deeper into the mountains of Alpine Allgäu. It wasn't the first time I had wandered off like this, especially if I'd had a drink or two. I was easily overwhelmed by bustling city environments and was often compelled by the sudden urge to escape: In the mid-90s, while living in London, I called into work sick, just for one day, but soon got bored and decided to roam the tube network. Seven days later my boss called me into his office and wanted to know why he had received a postcard from me, sent six days previously from the depths of northern France calling him a "dickhead." As soon as he mentioned it, I vaguely recalled a ferry trip and getting into an argument with a sock salesman from Birmingham but not much more.

Anyway, two or three hours after I had wandered onto a German train, whose destination I had not bothered to check, I found myself in a small, picture-postcard Bavarian village. It was like a kitsch, mid-century illustrated Christmas card with its glittery pillows of snow hanging over mediaeval roofs; heart shapes cut out of the hand-carved window shutters. I soon discovered that all return trains were cancelled due to the snow until morning, so I headed to the village pub—the only place where lights were on—where I resolved to have a drink and enquire about accommodation.

Despite my ignorance of the local dialect, which even my German colleagues in Munich would have deemed impenetrable, I somehow managed to order a beer. The waiter brought it to me, its foamy head as deep as the snow outside, and from him I also gleaned that, fittingly, there was no room at the inn, not that I cared: If it came to it, the local train station had been more inviting and cleaner than hotels I'd stayed in. The musty old pub was little more than a large wooden hut whose—let's be generous and call them *aromatic*—walls were steeped in centuries of maturing cheeses and dry-curing sausages, the latter of which hung precariously from the rafters along with scythes and other lethal farming equipment.

After a few moments of wondering how on earth I came to be in this 1940s animated Disney Pinocchio village, I heard screaming outside. I squinted out of the yellow-tinted bubbled glass to see what looked like a polar bear rush past the window. At first, I blamed the snow, altitude, and beer for the unexpected vision but seconds later, there was another polar bear. I paid up and left. Out on the street, I could hear the distant clamour of excited voices, so I headed in its general direction.

Echoing through the narrow streets came the sound of rhythmic clanking metal, like an army of marching hammers. A farming contraption of some description?

I turned a corner right into the path of a horde of striding beasts: seven feet tall, clad from head to foot in dirty white furs and skins with sharp horns framing their heads. These heavily bearded but faceless giants bore enormous cowbells —the size of overly-fed babies—around their waists, which they stimulated with regular pelvic thrusts in unison with others in their pack, or whatever the collective noun is for marauding otherworldly behemoths you don't ever want to meet in your life. The closest experience I'd had to this was bingeing *Lord of the Rings* boxsets, so I didn't have time to decode the encounter before the leading beast turned to me and raised an arm high above his head. I only realised there was something in his hand when I heard a whip of air and felt a sharp pain slice across my legs. Then I saw the tightly bound bundle of birch rods. Others in the pack followed suit and, without altering their course or pace, flogged me half a dozen times before they marched on, leaving me astounded and with one very fundamental question:

"What the actual fuck is going on?"

Stunned, I returned to the pub. The locals were avoiding eye contact with me; were they whispering about me?

In the bathroom, I pulled down my trousers and traced with a finger the raised, pinkish-red welts striped across my calves and thighs. I decided to brave the outside again simply because I couldn't comprehend what had just happened and needed further data. I mean, for Christ's sake; it was the 21st century; this was the stuff of folk-horror B-movies. Had I been drawn here by mysterious Fate, destined to be sacrificed in a rite to appease the local cheese deities? I didn't want to die simply because superstitious villagers hoped to ensure a successful range of dairy products.

Restricting myself to dark shop-front recesses, over the next hour I spied these colossal entities break ranks to chase villagers, especially boys and teenagers emboldened enough, like bullfighters, to goad their pursuers. The dark village streets were awash with the din of echoing bells and wails. I also discovered that the monstrous predators could be cunning, dampening their bells when stealthily hunting their unsuspecting prey. When cornered unawares, the young victims soon lost their swagger and were forced to kneel before the beasts who encircled them with their heavy groin bells thrusting louder and faster. And if the prey's contrition was not deemed adequate—if their hands were not clasped tightly enough in supplicating prayer—they were rained on by punishing birch rods, their shrieks (which, I detected, were sometimes tinged with distinct exhilaration), echoing across the mountain valley.

I later learned that this ritual is called, depending on which godforsaken nook of the Alps you find yourself in, *Klausentreiben. Klausjagen, Sünnekläuse* or *Chlausjagen*. The 'Klaus' part of the name is the Alpine equivalent of Claus, as in Santa Claus.

Yes: These shaggy brutes are Santa Claus, or rather his confederates. Not the jolly, benevolent, rose-cheeked, red- and white-clad grandfather we've come to associate with Christmas; this pagan entity predates its namesake Saint Nicholas and even Christianity itself. The traditional intention of the *Klausen* is to drive out evil winter spirits but, as history has shown us for time immemorial, such spirits only ever seem to conveniently reside in the least favoured members of the community. Apparently, a few decades ago, the annual *Klausen* ritual had to be suspended because the violence got out of hand.

Klausen belong in the tradition of *Krampus*, a demonic, old Central-European figure who accompanies Saint Nicholas. In Germany specifically he's also known as *Ruprecht* (once a common name for The Devil). While St. Nick hands out gifts to the good children, or rather the children who don't dare question God's infinite benevolence under threat of eternal, torturous damnation; it's the serpent-tongued, black-pelted, horned, goat-ish Krampus or impish Ruprecht who know if you've been bad or good, *so be good for goodness sake*. Those who don't heed the warning during the year may find themselves thrust into Krampus's *Butte* or *Kraxn*—damnation in the form of an imprisoning wicker basket clamped to his back.

Cowering, half-drunk in a rural village, miles, if not centuries, from anywhere, I inexplicably recalled after three decades, my school friend. Even with the karmic accident that had smashed his calculator (and fingers), I realized he would have been flogged and incarcerated in the basket-of-doom anyway, just for good measure; but I wondered what on earth I had done to warrant my lashing from the *Klausen*. What transgressions had I committed in the previous year to warrant such retribution? Is it possible that ancient pagan spirits somehow knew I had accidentally forgotten to ring through that small can of anchovies at the supermarket self-checkout last August, and subsequently decided against re-

imbursing the shop for my oversight? How the hell do ancient pagan spirits even know what a self-checkout is? I was pretty sure that such supernatural beings looked after crops, weather, and the welfare of hens, and had not suddenly developed an understanding of modern retail technologies such as bar- and QR-codes, wireless credit card confirmation, and the digital transaction of encrypted data. No, I began to comprehend that I had just been in the wrong place at the wrong time and my transgressions were still secretly confined to my own conscience.

Rubbing my by now stinging legs, I headed back to the train station, glancing over my shoulder the entire way. At least the lone, palely lit waiting room existed in the modern world. I'd try to sleep there until what I hoped would be the first train back to Munich at 7 a.m., but sleep was impossible on the hard, red plastic-moulded seats.

I texted my old friend. "Do you remember adding up the value of your Christmas presents?" For twenty-five years he'd worked in The City and was still a big fish in international finance, even after playing a bit part in the 2008 global recession. I received a reply ten minutes later: A crying-with-laughter emoji. "What made you remember that?" he asked. "Father Christmas just tried to murder me," I replied. Back came a confused-face emoji. I typed that I was sorry if I'd woken him. He replied that I hadn't: He was in Barbados making the deal of a lifetime. If all went well, he said, he'd be able to retire within the year. Being on the Naughty List clearly hadn't diminished his life in any way.

Around 1 A.M., the waiting room doors burst open and in staggered a *Klaus*. His birch rod was frayed and splintered from enthusiastic use. I sat bolt upright, compelled to behave, and panicked: Do ancient pagan entities have favourite seats, and was I sitting in this one's? Apparently not: The *Klaus* slumped heavily into another seat—or rather three seats, so bulky was the fur.

He sat hunched over and swaying, breathing heavily like a bison I'd once seen, before slowly prising off the head section of his costume. Beneath it was a man about twenty years old—a strapping farm boy type—his red face shiny with sweat, his hair plastered to his steaming forehead. He was clearly fantastically drunk. His glassy eyes swam in my general direction, and he slurred something in mountain dialect. When he realized I wasn't local, he dismissed me with a wave.

"American?" he eventually managed to mutter.

"English," I said.

His response was to violently throw up onto the floor between his spread legs. Realising that the deluge had sprayed his ankles and feet, he swore, then struggled awkwardly to remove his soiled boots, which he threw angrily out of the waiting room door into the snow.

Leaning back and trying painfully to regain his breath, he flung out his heavy legs to stop himself from toppling over. The lad was in palpable discomfort. It was then that I saw, poking out of the dense fur at the end his unsteady legs, his comparatively small feet. He was wearing novelty socks decorated with images of Garfield the orange cartoon cat.

"Garfield," I said when I felt confident enough. The *Klaus* scowled at me blurrily.

"Garfield," he growled resignedly, as if Garfield were somehow responsible for his profound intoxication, and then he threw up again, this time all down his furry costume. A moment later the dishevelled *Klaus* wearily raised his tattered birch rod one last time and resentfully swatted his own socked foot, or rather the cynical, heavy-eyed cartoon cat on it.

It was then that I understood this *Klaus* had foolishly assumed he had been at the apex of the disciplinary hierarchy—the punisher, not the punished—and yet his own personal *kismet* had somehow found him in the form of extravagant quantities of alcohol and Garfield: Garfield the karmic judge; Garfield the cosmic punisher.

Perhaps ancient peoples had got it right: No matter how exemplary our conduct, righteous Fate will come along one day and give us a good thrashing—no matter which moral boxes we think we've checked. Christmas good and bad lists be damned; if even nasty pagan Santa and his vomiting accomplices can't escape the random punishments meted out by primaeval spirits, supreme beings, crop deities, and even the almighty gods of cheese and novelty cartoon socks, what chance do any of us stand? ◼

"I should probably mention my barbed penis."

"Tell me that doesn't make you hungry."

"Still fresh. We're getting close."

Tyson Cole
is a cartoonist, illustrator, and graphic designer living in Utah. See more work on Instagram: @tysoncole.3000. **B**

MarshallNotFunny
@marshallcartoon
Well thank heavens for that...I never could draw Liz Truss.

Crybaby

*Two Canadian gnomes equal
one Terminator.*

On her way out the door, my wife reminded me that there were diapers in the bottom of the stroller. Also, that our oldest had refused breakfast—"stay on top of that." And if our daughter, who had recently turned four, refused to cooperate, she could talk to Mommy on the phone. "Your cell is charged, right?"

I chuckled and gave my wife a hug. "Honey, there's nothing to worry about, I've got this." Relieved by my confidence, she let out a long, deep sigh, rubbed her temples, and rapidly blinked. "Whatever," she said eventually, then left for the day to visit her sister in Brooklyn.

I closed the door. My wife was by all accounts a wonderful mother, but with one problem: she worried too much. Sure, the kids could be trouble. But they were kids, weren't they? They need to make mistakes. It's how they learn.

As these insights streamed forth, I heard a fist connecting with flesh in the kid's room, followed by a shout. I stood passively and listened, waiting for them to settle the dispute on their own.

Then I heard another fist-on-flesh smack, to the chest maybe, or the belly. Then came what I immediately recognized as a large plastic train careening into a wall. The next sound was tougher—my best guess was my daughter falling on the plastic train, then that train flipping up and hitting her back in the face. But enough was enough, and it was time to see how good I was at guessing.

When I arrived in the kids' room, well, it wasn't pretty. They were at each other's throats. But then, after taking stock and inhaling deeply, I told them they were acting like absolute monsters. I said this using my "Daddy is angry and screaming at you" voice. And for whatever reason that made it much, much worse.

Fighting. Yelling. Spitting. Crying. Spiraling. It went on like this for hours. It became clear that I was entirely powerless to stop them, so I tried a different approach.

I put the screaming baby in his crib, so he could take a nap or whatever. I plopped the older two in front of the TV and put on *PAW Patrol*. I retreated to the kitchen, where the sound of pups extinguishing a fire drowned out the baby's cries. And as the baby lost gusto and things finally quieted down, I whipped out my phone and took a much-needed break from the strains of parenting.

I had forgotten all about lunch, and boy was I hungry. I went to open the fridge, but something was stuck in front, blocking the light.

To my complete surprise, out of the fridge tumbled two small men. They were approximately the size of microwave ovens and wore identical green jumpsuits. On the breast pocket of one was an image of a moose, on the other a… hockey puck? In their tiny hands each held a blazingly sharp machete.

These gnomes were super-agile; falling out of the fridge, they each did a few somersaults on the linoleum and came up in a fighting stance. I held back a yelp, hoping not to disturb the baby's nap.

"It's him, eh?" said the one with the moose patch on his pocket. He spat on my kitchen floor. "You disgusting piece of human garbage!"

"Do I—know you?" I sputtered.

"It's time to act. For a better future, eh?" said Moose.

"For a better future—eh!" said Puck, raising his machete above his head.

Michael Pershan *is Deputy Editor of The American Bystander.*

MILK
MILK
MAYO
PICKLES
CHATFIELD

"Take money," I said, my voice cracking, as I opened my wallet and realized I was out of cash. "Or my debit card, I'll give you the PIN. What about Israel bonds? Do you take those? They're in a shoebox in the closet."

"Silence! There is one thing we want, and it is not Israel bonds." Puck raised his machete even higher, grinning murderously.

Suddenly, I understood. I looked

"Go ahead," Puck said, "crying helps." Then Puck turned to me. "Go back in time, eliminate the dictator, that's our mission. Stop the war before it even has a chance to start," he said, and then gestured widely. "This is why we're here."

I wanted to tell my kids to turn that idiotic TV off—Daddy needed quiet to think. But I didn't dare; these Canadians were clearly as crazy as they were short. "You think *I'm* going to turn into

"Unless we act now!" shouted Puck, shaking his machete.

"This is insane," I said. "You're both insane."

"In the future, your shittiness as a father is legend," Moose said. "Everyone knows the stories. They are repeated at underground weddings and clandestine circumcisions."

"Gatherings of two or more are strictly prohibited," Puck chimed in. Then

tim Hunt

straight into their eyes. "Kidnappers," I whispered. Then, in as hard and menacing a voice as I could muster while wearing soft pants, I hissed, "Here's a word of warning: don't lay a fucking finger on my children, or I will *hunt you down and make you suffer*."

The little men looked at each other. And then, they started laughing. Big, hearty laughs. Much deeper laughs than I thought could come out of bodies that small. I'd been maximum threatening and they were *tickled*. Oh shit.

"Worried about his kids?!"

Moose and Puck just kept laughing, to the point where it stopped being sinister and became irritating.

"Tell me what is going on!" I wanted to shout this, but I choked it into a strangled whisper—the last thing I needed was to wake the baby.

Moose took a deep breath and wiped his eyes. "I guess we can tell him, eh?" He stood up a little straighter. "My colleague and I are part of the Canadian Imperial Time Squad."

Puck chimed in. "We are here to take your life, eh? To prevent the rise of a terrible dictator."

"The worst ever," Moose said. "The future is a terrible place. Endless war. The climate crisis allowed his rise. And then, the slaughter began…" Moose's voice broke. The other agent placed his hand on his shoulder.

some sort of dictator?"

Again, they laughed.

"Quit laughing! Two mini-Canadians break into my home, hide in my fridge—"

"Right, OK," Moose said. "No laughing." They both tried to compose themselves.

"Yes, let's be professional," Puck said, pulling out a piece of paper. "I have here a warrant declaring—but look at his face, he still thinks it's him!" They collapsed into fresh gales of mirth.

Just then, I heard my kids in the other room. "Give me the remote or I'll scream in your ear!" my son said. My daughter shouted back that she wouldn't. "Give! It! Now!" he screamed directly into her ear. Something about how he shouted—it sounded almost German.

The two gnomes heard it, too, and it made their laughter dry up in an instant.

"Him?" I said. "But he's just a kid."

"Our quantum scientists have flawlessly reconstructed the events leading to your son's rise to power," Moose said. He took an instrument from his pocket; on its screen was a rapidly vibrating line. "This squiggle means we are close to the crucial moment. The moment when he becomes a broken individual, broken beyond repair, beyond imagination. And it is due to you and your very, very bad parenting."

added sourly, "Unless they're rallies for 'Dear Leader.'"

Moose continued. "Books detailing your failures were quite popular as cautionary gifts to expectant parents. Your son became enraged and outlawed them. But people still made their own, so he banned paper."

"Even then, the tales lived on," Puck said. "People passed them down orally. They declaimed you in verse."

"Like *The Iliad*," Moose said, "except about how shitty you are at parenting."

"Your failures are the basis of our entire culture," said Puck. "Everybody has a favorite shitty-Michael story! Mine's 'That time when Michael yelled at his kids and then hid in the kitchen.'"

"Without giving them lunch," Moose said, hissing the words disdainfully.

"It was an exhausting morning," I said. "My wife went to Brooklyn, and they were so bad for me."

"Boo-fucking-hoo! Daddy had a bwad mowning," Moose said in an unnecessarily mean baby voice.

"Well, thirty-two years later, your boy personally chopped off nearly all my digits!" Puck spat, jabbing my chest with a one-fingered hand. "All because you didn't want to deal with your kids' drama, you piece of fatherly scum!"

Moose wedged himself between us. "Puck! Remember your training," he said. "We knew he was going to suck. Don't let that compromise the mission.

Let the machete do the talking, eh."

"Eh," Puck said, in an apologetic tone. I could hear, in the other room, that my son was sitting on my daughter's head. She was clearly in pain. Any louder and they would certainly wake the baby. Who would have to deal with that? Me. Ugh, this morning was the worst.

Moose read my mind. "Soon, the boy will shout at his sister and wake the baby. And that's when you cross the final line."

"You give him a time out, you rat-bastard," Puck whispered.

"Won't he deserve it?" I said, weakly.

"And then, through tears, he will ask you why only he is being punished, how is this his fault? Then you will lose your temper at him. Again. You will yell. But not because of anything he did. Just because you are a bad dad and a giant infant, surpassing any child in your selfish immaturity."

Puck stepped forward. "Your death will ensure that this line is not crossed."

"Hold on a sec." My mind was racing a mile-a-minute; this was a lot to take in. "Before you kill me, let's just make sure everything matches up. I mean, this stuff is complicated. Maybe some other dude is the cause of this mess. You'll have sat in that fridge for nothing."

"Our quantum scientists—"

"Have you considered Hitler? I know who Hitler is, which means you didn't go back and kill him. If you have a time machine, why not start with him?" I asked.

Moose just shook his head.

"Clueless, just clueless," Moose said.

Puck gave me an icy stare. "There is no comparison between your son and Hitler."

"He's like triple Hitler," Moose added. "On a good day."

I had to play for time, it was my only move left. "I apologize if this is insensitive," I asked, "but why are you so short? Are all the people in the future this small?"

"Wow. He went there."

"And launching into it with that faux-polite apology. That's another shitty-Michael story for the file. Shall I remember it, or will you?" Moose asked.

"Oh, I'll remember it," said Puck.

Moose said, "Our size is a consequence of our work. I don't have time to explain it more. If there is a hell, ask Satan about 'time dilation.' Basically, each mission, you get shorter."

"The blood of our victims has made us small," said Puck, smiling.

"And now, time to die." Both raised their machetes.

Just then, a shout rang from the living room. As these Canadians had foretold, my son pulled his sister's hair, and then pushed her off the couch. There was a loud thud and then a scream. And then, from the back of the apartment, the baby cried.

Really? The kids chose now to wake the baby? Just as I was starting to make some progress with the Canuck gnome death squad?

"*Stop it!*" I shouted into the living room. "Stop! Or I swear…"

I didn't get to finish the sentence.

"Quickly! Now!" I heard the pleasant sound of their blades whistling through the air, humming together.

In the end, there was no pain.

Only darkness.

I was in the kitchen, fiddling with my phone while the kids watched TV in the living room. It was their second, maybe tenth *PAW Patrol* in a row, I couldn't say for sure. The baby was finally asleep after I'd let him cry in his crib. On my phone I was watching videos of dolphins who had grown deeply attached to their trainers. The dolphins had learned, in time, to kiss these caretakers. I wondered if there was a dolphin out there that might do that to me.

Just then, I realized I was starving. I opened the fridge. To my surprise, out tumbled two small men wearing green jumpsuits. They were armed with machetes. They were quite short.

"Let's give it another shot!" said the one with a moose on his pocket.

"You said that last time," said the one with a hockey puck on his uniform, doing a few somersaults on his way out the fridge.

"What is going on?" I asked.

"I think it's your turn, eh?" said Puck, coming up in a fighting stance.

"Thank you, I lost track," said Moose, doing several flips across my kitchen floor.

I wanted to tell them something, to ask them to be quieter, to explain that I couldn't think straight right now, I just needed a minute to rest and eat while the kids watched TV. But I didn't have the chance.

There was no pain.

Then, darkness.

I opened the fridge and out tumbled two extremely small men armed with machetes.

"Let's try stabbing together this time, eh?" said the one with a puck on his pocket, mid-air.

"Simul-stabbing, a good idea," said the other.

"On the count of three."

"One."

"Two."

"Hold on now," I said.

"Three."

"Are you guys Canad—"

"Are we just going to run suicides again all day?."

There was really quite a bit of pain. Then, darkness.

Kids! TV! Baby! Crib! Hungry! Fridge! Dudes! Eh! Stab! Pain! Bleed! Bleed! Die!
Darkness.

I opened the fridge and out tumbled two extremely small men in green jumpsuits. They were, to reiterate, extremely small, each roughly as large as a pineapple. In their hands were blazing sharp machetes, which they gripped tightly though the huge blades were much larger than their bodies. They seemed awfully tired.
The taller of the two, who had a moose on his uniform, spoke in a high-pitched squawk. I couldn't make out what he was saying, so I leaned closer. I think he said that he was going to kill me on account of how I was such a shitty dad, that he and his buddy had killed me many times before, and that they would keep killing me for the rest of time if that's what it took to prevent Triple-Hitler and alter their terrible future.

At least I think that's what he said. He was very hard to hear.

From the other room, my son shouted at his sister. "Give me the remote or I'll scream in your ear!" he said, but my daughter refused. Any louder and they would certainly wake the baby.

I sighed. Everyone was so unhappy in this apartment: my kids, these two tiny killers (a strong instinct told me they were Canadian), and most of all, me. I didn't need to be told I was failing as a parent. All morning I had made everyone miserable. That's why I was here, hiding in the kitchen, giving everyone a break from myself.

I thought of what I could say to get these pocket assassins to leave me alone. I could think of nothing. They hated me and there was nothing to do about it. I just wanted another chance, but I didn't know how to get one. Suddenly, I started to cry. The tears came in big sobs that I couldn't stop. They came out much louder than I thought they would.

So loud, in fact, that I woke the baby. Everybody was making noise now. The kids were screaming, the baby was crying, and I was sobbing too, but also the two guys were squawking at each other with their tiny voices.

The assassins were having a disagreement. The one with a tiny puck on his shirt kept gesturing at me with his weapon. The one with the moose shrugged his shoulders while pointing to his fancy-looking instrument. Eventually, Puck threw his machete down. It rattled on my tile floor as he crossed his arms and pouted.

Moose motioned for me to bend over and look at his instrument's futuristic screen. I wiped my tears and tried to listen to his cartoonishly high voice. There was something important happening, he said, something they had never yet seen in all their attempts.

"It is the closest we've ever gotten," he told me. "Triple Hitler Threat Reading is near zero."

"Wow," I sniffled, pretending to understand. "Just great."

Moose told me that to have changed the odds, I must have somehow realized something that made me a less-shitty parent. I nodded, but only because he still had the machete. I have a policy of agreeing with anything machete-holders say. Anyway, all I had realized was that I couldn't control how these sad little people felt about me, only how I treated them. What did that have to do with parenting?

"The vibrations are clear," he continued. "Our fate is no longer certain. The Triple Hitler may never arise."

"And if he does?" Puck said with a smile, "we'll just come back and kill you again."

With that, the two men shook my finger and somersaulted back into the fridge. There was a bright flash followed by a *frzap!* Then, they were gone for good. The mayonnaise wobbled a little, then stopped.

Now it was just me and the kids again. The older two had missed out on the whole machete thing and were fighting on the couch as if nothing had happened. The baby was shrieking like a maniac. The noise made my head spin, and I felt myself growing tense and upset at their screaming and cruelty, that old familiar feeling.

I went back to the kitchen and opened the fridge. I checked the produce drawers and all the shelves. No tiny Canadians, as far as I could tell. I removed a bowl of cold macaroni and scooped it onto three plates. I picked up three miserable, screaming children and shoved plates of pasta in front of each. I squirted ketchup on their pasta, and they shoveled it into their mouths. And I, their caretaker, smiled at them while they ate, until our tears had dried and we all had gotten what we needed. **B**

"The piped-in spa music makes all the difference."

Sarah Morrissette *was raised on a Greek island and a hippie commune; after that start she has tried, only semi-successfully, to "blend in." Now in Vienna, her work appears in* **Alta, Air Mail, Funny Times** *and many other venues.*

B

"I hear someone here likes The Spider Man…"

"Oh fuck yes. Let's make these fuckers live for-fucking-eve

"You wanna take this o-u-t-s-i-d-e?"

Asher Perlman (@asherperlman) *is an Emmy-nominated, Peabody-award winning comedian. He is a writer for* **The Late Show with Stephen Colbert**, *and a performer anywhere that will have him.*

NOTES FROM A SMALL PLANET

Boys and bargains with me and Chlorine • *By Rick Geary*

ANOTHER WEEKEND AT THE ROUTE 27 MERCHANDISE COMPLEX.

AS ALWAYS, MY VENUE FOR FUN, LOVE... AND HEARTBREAK.

MY FRIEND CHLORINE AND I CRUISE AROUND, CHECKING OUT BOYS AND BARGAINS.

A LOT OF SHODDY STUFF ON DISPLAY THESE DAYS... IN BOTH CATEGORIES!

THAT BOY-IN-A-SUIT SHOWED UP AGAIN. HE SURE IS CUTE!

SHOULD I GO AFTER HIM? I HAVE BEEN HURT BEFORE.

WE'VE MADE THE INITIAL "EYE CONTACT."

CHLORINE SAYS I SHOULD TAKE A RISK AND NAB HIM... EASY FOR HER TO SAY.

IN THE MEANTIME, AS A PROMOTION FOR THE COMPLEX...

A FIGHT BETWEEN WILD BEASTS IS STAGED 40 FEET IN THE AIR.

BLOOD AND FUR RAIN UPON SHOPPERS... A VERY FESTIVE ATMOSPHERE.

AS A BONUS, RARE CARNIVORES ROAM THE AISLES OF PARTICIPATING RETAILERS.

WHEN NEXT I SEE THE BOY-IN-A-SUIT, HE'S BUT A MOUND OF SHREDDED FLESH.

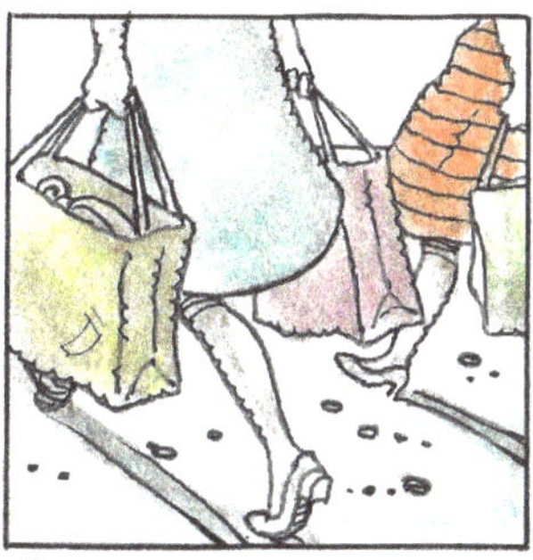

SO PERHAPS IT'S JUST AS WELL I DIDN'T PURSUE HIM.

THE MERCHANDISE COMPLEX IS NOW A GUTTED RUIN — AS ARE MY DREAMS.

WHAT AM I DOING HERE?

How Low Can You Sink? My trip to the Titanic • By Mike Reiss

My wife and I like danger. And by "my wife and I," I mean just my wife, not me, not even a little. People know this about us, so my friend Jay called with an invitation: "You guys wanna come to a party tonight? There's a good chance you will be killed."

This was not some cute murder mystery dinner party—this was the real thing. They were having a cocktail reception for Vladimir Putin's number one enemy. He was a marked man. We were excited until Jay added, "While you're at the party, I advise you not to eat or drink anything." This might have been a deal-breaker: I don't mind getting shot or blown up, but I go to a party to eat.

Another friend told us about a guy who took passengers on deep dives in his home-made submarines. This sounded like a good way to get killed, so my wife asked for the man's name. It was Stockton Rush.

They say name is destiny. Martin Short really is short. Fats Domino was pretty fat. And Cedric the Entertainer… looks like a Cedric. So when your name is Stockton Rush, you are fated to a life of adventure. Mr. Rush is as handsome and suave as a soap opera doctor. He'd had every career an eight year-old boy could dream of: airline pilot, rocket scientist, inventor and now submarine captain.

MIKE REISS

is Intrepid Traveler for *The American Bystander*.

Our Intrepid Traveler 370 miles off the coast of Newfoundland, and two and a half miles straight down.

Our voyages with Captain Rush started small and grew, well, titanic. Our first trip left from an exotic port off a mysterious island known as…Staten. A hundred miles off Staten Island is Hudson Canyon, an underwater chasm the size of the Grand Canyon. We were going to dive it, in Rush's home-made sub. It was gleaming white and streamlined, like a Star Wars TIE Fighter or a high-end vape pen. The viewport was a giant acrylic eyeball, surrounded by spotlights and lasers. A towboat pulled the submarine, bobbing and bouncing as we headed out to sea.

The most dangerous part of riding this sub, the bit no one put a lot of thought into, was getting in the damn thing. They simply leaned a six-foot kitchen ladder against the floating submarine. You had to scramble up the ladder as it bobbed with the waves, leap over to a tiny entry hatch on top, then plunge blindly into the sub, dropping six feet into darkness.

Once you were in, it was groovy: cool, dimly lit, quiet. The sub's interior was about the same as a mini-van; it would seat five, if there were seats. Instead, five of us spread out on the carpeted floor: pilot, co-pilot, my wife, myself, and one other rich stupid tourist with

a death wish. We sank noiselessly, peacefully to the bottom of the sea. One thousand feet down, the ocean floor looked like the landscape from a Road Runner cartoon: miles of sand, oddly shaped rocks, and the occasional coral branching out like a saguaro cactus. It was amazing.

It was only after we returned that they told us we were the first people ever to go down there! I was the Neil Armstrong of Hudson Canyon. This would be great, except I don't want to be the Neil Armstrong of anything! I want to be the Harrison Schmitt—the twelfth and final man on the moon. He didn't go up till they got all the kinks out.

But Stockton Rush was emboldened by this success, and he wanted to go somewhere deeper. Twelve times deeper. He wanted to take a sub to the *Titanic*, two and a half miles down. And my wife wanted us to go with him.

Two years later, Denise and I were standing on a dock in Newfoundland. Out in the harbor was the ship that would take us to the very spot where the *Titanic* sank. A rubber speedboat pulled up to take us to the ship, when the skipper realized, "Oh man, I forgot the life jackets!" This of course, was the same mistake the *Titanic* made.

Here we were: prosperous tourists risking our lives on an untested vehicle to see where other prosperous tourists lost their lives on an untested vehicle. Whatever—this was my wife's dream and my birthday gift to her. I had no idea what the trip cost and Denise wouldn't tell me. She told all our friends though, who would look at me and go, "You are some good husband," or "Wow! What a sap!" Both were correct.

Captain Rush built an all-new sub for this dive. It sat on the deck of the ship, white and bulbous like an Imperial Storm Trooper's helmet from, again, Star Wars. The porthole had to be much smaller—it was the size and shape of a window on a washing machine. In fact, that's where it may have come from.

The sub looked super-cool from the front. But in the back, it had a bunch of Styrofoam blocks randomly strapped on, to improve buoyancy. They said this was super high-tech styrofoam, but it looked the stuff every 80's stereo came packed in. There were also two flotation tanks that looked like bulging eyes, and a landing pad that resembled a gaping mouth. The sub looked scared to death. So was I.

The launch of this new sub had many setbacks before getting to this point: there was the pandemic. There was bad weather and rough seas. Once, the sub got struck by lightning, frying the electronics. On a test dive, a system failure trapped everyone inside it for 27 hours. And finally the submarine's toilet broke. This was troubling news, since the toilet was basically a potty seat—two pieces, no moving parts.

They were explaining all these setbacks to us on a Powerpoint presentation when the computer died too. Uh-oh.

Then they brought out waivers for us to sign. Here are some highlights:

"While diving below the ocean surface I will be subject to extreme pressure and any failure of the vessel could cause severe injury or death."

"I will be exposed to risks associated with high-pressure gases, pure oxygen, and high voltage systems which could lead to injury, disability and death."

"If I am injured I may not receive immediate medical attention."

"Welcome aboard!"

We sailed for two days, three hundred miles into the North Atlantic. Many on the crew were Newfoundlanders, a people so insular they still had the Irish accent of their distant ancestors. They'd also never heard of *The Simpsons*, the show I'd been working on for three decades. The one writing credit I had that excited them

was *ALF*, a series that was canceled thirty-five years ago. Here's a verbatim exchange:

SEA COOK (*IRISH LILT*): Alf was some character. Can I call you Alfie?
ME: I'd rather you didn't.
SEA COOK: Ah, you're a funny one, Uncle Alfie.
ME: So now I'm your uncle?

I emailed Paul Fusco, the creator of *ALF*, to tell him there was a pocket of die-hard fans onboard this ship. He wrote back, "Next trip, sell merchandise."

The day finally arrived—we were anchored two miles above the wreck of the *Titanic*. They outfitted my wife and me in matching navy blue flight suits. It was supposed to make us feel like crew members, but I just felt like an idiot. It's like when you put a fire chief's helmet

The Titan, pop-eyed with fear. Yes, those white blocks are Styrofoam.

on a five year-old. He may look cute, but he won't be putting out any fires.

We were now ready to board the submarine—we just had to take a Covid test. I passed mine. Denise failed hers. My wife, who had traveled to every continent since the pandemic began, had avoided catching Covid for two and a half years. But somehow she'd contracted it on this tiny boat in the North Atlantic.

Captain Rush said, "Sorry Denise, you can't take the trip. But Mike, you can still go!"

I said, "I don't wanna go!"

It's as if Neil Armstrong were getting ready to go to the moon when he came down with the flu. So NASA tells his wife, "You can go to the moon instead."

Yes, I'm comparing myself to Mrs. Neil Armstrong. But at Denise's insistence, I got on that sub and began a two-hour

descent straight to the bottom of the sea.

The number of disasters preceding this trip was pretty amazing when you see how simple a mini-sub is. It's basically a car that you drunkenly drove into the ocean. It sinks like a stone until it finally hits bottom. When you want to come up, you drop some of your weights, and pop to the surface like a cork. That's it: sink like a stone, pop up like a cork.

If they want to tilt the sub down, the pilot yells, "Everyone pile into the front. Hurry, hurry." To tilt it up: "Get in the back, move it, move it!"

To steer the sub, the pilot uses an Xbox game controller. I don't mean it looks like one—it's an actual joystick from a gaming system.

How can I describe my voyage to the bottom of the sea? It was…boring. The ocean here is pretty empty, so there was nothing to see out the porthole. I actually fell asleep. And if you want a shock, try waking up from a nap thinking you're home in bed, and realizing you're in a steel tube, two miles under water, and sinking.

We touched bottom amid the usual assortment of catastrophes. We were nowhere near the *Titanic*. There were underwater currents pushing us farther and farther in the wrong direction. The sonar wasn't working and the compass kept flopping from east to west, north to south. There was also a time crunch. We had started late and there was a hurricane rolling in on the surface. Just another day in the life of Captain Stockton Rush.

A navigator on the surface was sending us directions but they did not conform to what we were seeing. The Russian science officer kept radioing the surface: "We need better directions. Switch to the B map."

The crew on the surface replied, "What is 'the B map'?"

There were five of us in the sub, and four were working on the navigation. I was just 180 pounds of Jewish ballast.

The Russian kept up the pressure. "You must switch to the B map immediately!"

The crew responded, "There is no 'B map'! We don't know what you're talking about!"

Finally, just minutes before we had to give up, we saw it: the bow of the *Titanic*.

We had twenty minutes to snap selfies with the famous parts, the bits you've seen in a million documentaries: the railing, the prow, the anchor. It wasn't overwhelming, it wasn't underwhelming. It was whelming.

Just prior to this trip, we'd been to Vegas, where every show has a VIP package: pay fifty bucks extra, and you get to go backstage afterwards. You shake hands with the star, you get your photo with them, you get the hell out of there. I'd wound up on the *Titanic* VIP package. This wasn't an adventure, it was a photo op.

The only real danger came in the last minute of the voyage. As the sub was being hoisted back onto the ship, the whole thing flipped vertical. Everything in the sub—computers, phones, five people and their sandwiches—crashed in a heap at the bottom of the sub. A trip to the *Titanic* ended in disaster.

The next day Captain Rush had another dive and it went perfectly. They had two solid hours to explore the wreckage, from stem to stern, from starboard to the other one. It was a glorious adventure and I missed it all. I'd stayed behind on the ship, ministering to my Covid-y wife. She was quarantined in her stateroom, sitting in the dark, demanding food: "Bring me fruit!"

I ran down two flights to the galley, loaded trays with watermelon, and ran them back up to her. But it was never enough. For a sick and slender woman, her appetite was ravenous: "MORE FRUIT!"

It was like serving a dragon. A vegan dragon.

Denise is already planning a return trip, so we can visit the *Titanic* together. That trip I never wanted to take? I'm taking it twice. Whatever it cost me, I'll be paying double.

Only when we were sailing home did I realize the import of what I'd done. Captain Rush told me, "More people have been in outer space than have done what you did yesterday." A passenger from Guadalajara became the first Mexican ever to reach the *Titanic*. As for me, I became the first *ALF* writer to get there. Take that, Mrs. Neil Armstrong!

DAYBREAK AND A CANDLE-END

Ron answers one of the pressing questions of our Age. • *By Ron Barrett*

Where Do Babies Come From?

KIDS IN SCHOOL HAD THEIR OWN BABY ORIGIN THEORIES

ANOTHER PAGE TORN FROM THE LIFE OF RON BARRETT

P.S. MUELLER THINKS LIKE THIS

The cartoonist/broadcaster/writer is always walking around, looking at stuff • By P.S. Mueller

P.S. MUELLER is Staff Liar of *The American Bystander.*

BY QUENTIN HARDY

IN CONCLUSION

Goodbye '22! So long sweet, adieu bitter / We're still not in shape, but at least we quit Twitter!

Each month has holidays, a host,
December, though, can boast the most.
Kwanzaa, Hanukkah, and Christmas,
Advent, Bodhi Day, and Solstice.
Boxing Day, and Omisoka,
One for mourning Zarathustra!

Salute them all! But we believe
There's nothing quite like New Year's Eve.
Toll out the Old! Ring in the New!
And praise that we're past '22.

We had our elections, our polls, and our coups:
In Ouagadougou they managed two coups!
Don't laugh at their couping: Oh say, can't you see
Our own Jan. 6th couping will soon hit Year Three.

And while we're on voting, (which sure beats a *putsch*)
Recall Euroviz champ, Orchestra Kalush.
Their rap was about a Ukrainian mom,
We doubt Mr. Putin thought that was da bomb.

Last Feb, Dear Old Vlad rolled his tanks in Ukraine
For two weeks at most he did plan to remain.
Still there in December, for much to his shock
He met a tough comic—we don't mean Chris Rock.

Zelinsky looked out at the Russians arrayed
The troops drunk and surly, their tires decayed.
"We're in for a long one," he said with a sniff,
"But I like our odds, folks—I don't see Will Smith."

We prayed hard for peace till our lips became sore…
And Denmark and Nunavut ended their war!
Miracles do happen, though sometimes they're small.
Like how we had birthdays, us each and us all.

In England, Queen Bess tottled to her last bed,
Then Truss failed to outlast an old lettuce head.
The reign of King Charles, before it began,
Encountered rebellion: His kid and Meagan.

Conditions back here, too, were also "sub-neato."
Recall jurisprudence from Samuel Alito.

Doc Oz, QAnon, and our glorious right wing,
At least we came fourth at the games in Beijing.

In crypto the crashes continued to vex
As young SBF erased his FTX.
Chastened and hustled from penthouse to cage,
A WTF Ponzi, our WFH age.

(Last year was for gender, the hirs, theirs, and hims,
While this business year was for new acronyms.)
Set that bit aside though, and Business was Great
-Resign and -Reshuffle, some "Great-" terms to date.

Great Reset, Great Rethink (it's quite the obsession),
Great Remorse, Great Breakup (that gets "Great" de-
pressin').
The stock market, meantime, it went down the spout,
And Elon bought Twitter—how's that working out?

But if you liked records, here's listicle heaven:
Dinesh Sunar's backflips, done blind, 27.
• Herr Styles' "As It Was," Number One, fifteen weeks.
• Subpoenas for Donald, as high as his cheeks.

• El Messi found gold on the green turf of Qatar.
• "KPOP" flopped on Broadway with barely a mutter.
• While Yulimar Rojas, he triple-jumped faster,
• And Taylor the Swift destroyed ol' Ticketmaster.

Celebrity couples! Hey, Bennifer's back!
While Johnny and Amber both testified smack.
Kim K. went and shredded poor Marilyn's Dress
And Ye did much worse to his rep and success.

But there were small blessings, like VR and Wordle,
The Hadron Collider, Madonna's new girdle,
The Webb telescope and Top Gun in redux,
And mostly we skipped Avatar, monkeypox.

And so to a New Year, in power and passion,
We spin 'round the Sun faster than we imagine.
Each day is a gift, and a tale that reveals
How '23's going—For that, all the feels. B

QUENTIN HARDY *was a journalist at* **The Wall Street Journal**, **Forbes**, *and* **The New York Times**, *right up to the minute the world stopped making any goddamn sense. He now works at Google.*